POLICY AND PRAC⊤
NUMBER ELEVEN

Death, Dying and

D1343155

POLICY AND PRACTICE IN HEALTH AND SOCIAL CARE

POLICY AND PRACTICE IN HEALTH AND SOCIAL CARE

SERIES EDITORS

JOYCE CAVAYE and **ALISON PETCH**

Death, Dying and Bereavement: Issues for Practice

Dr Jacqueline H. Watts

Senior Lecturer and Staff Tutor in Health and Social Care at the Open University

Published by
Dunedin Academic Press Ltd
Hudson House
8 Albany Street
Edinburgh EH1 3QB
Scotland

ISBN: 978-1-906716-08-0
ISSN 1750-1407

British Library Cataloguing in Publication data
A catalogue record for this book is available from the British Library

Typeset by Makar Publishing Production, Edinburgh
Printed in the United Kingdom by Cpod, Trowbridge, Wiltshire
Printed on paper from sustainable resources

Mixed Sources
Product group from well-managed
forests and other controlled sources
www.fsc.org Cert no. TT-COC-2082
© 1996 Forest Stewardship Council
FSC

Dedication

This book is dedicated to the memory of
Phillip Dummett Haynes,
my beloved cousin

Contents

Series Editors' Introduction

In the words of this volume's author, 'death has become a behind-the-scenes activity'. The purpose of this contribution to the Policy and Practice in Health and Social Care series is therefore to put death and dying centre stage and to explore the ethical and practice dilemmas that arise as we strive to find an appropriate balance between the opportunities of medical advance and the ambitions to achieve, wherever possible, what could be defined as a 'good death'. We are reminded also of the importance of recognising and responding to the needs of the bereaved, and of the role for counselling and mutual help groups.

Jackie Watts highlights the changing trends in both cause and place of death and illustrates the diversity of cultural and religious responses. She explores what is meant by palliative care and how it is being currently implemented both in Scotland and elsewhere. She outlines the development of hospice care from its traditional building-based model to the current focus on extending the hospice philosophy into care homes and into people's own homes while addressing the need for greater diversity in the groups having access to palliative or hospice care. She also examines the interpretation of spiritual care, in its widest sense, and provides an understanding of the stages of grief and of the experience of mourning.

A focus of this volume is the identification of the key skills that can enhance practice. Critical is the need for good communication, both with the individual and family members and with the range of professionals involved. Multi-professional and multi-disciplinary contact needs to be of the highest order. Particularly important to health and social care practice is what can be termed disenfranchised grief, grief that may not be acknowledged or sanctioned. The hope is that this volume will go some way to encouraging a more open and differentiated response to a universal situation.

Dr Joyce Cavaye
Faculty of Health and Social Care, The Open University in Scotland, Edinburgh

Professor Alison Petch
*Director, **research in practice for adults**, Dartington Hall Trust, Totnes, Devon*

Acknowledgements

The topic of this book has been a key theme in my writing and research over recent years but the encouragement to write this volume has come principally from Joyce Cavaye, one of the series editors. Joyce has shown absolute faith in me in this endeavour and I am very grateful for her support. Alison Petch, as the second editor of this series, has given me invaluable advice and has helped me shape and re-shape the narrative to appeal to a wide readership. I have much appreciated her constructive and direct approach.

The ongoing interest of special friends Yvonne Gordon, Yvonne Dutch, Michelle Esterman and Susan Fulcher in my writing projects sustains me in ways hard to describe, but they know how much it means to me.

Finally, the support of Tony, Halina and Lauren Watts, my treasured family, has made all the difference to the craft of thinking and writing. Our fun, laughter and holidays together have helped anchor me during the past year in which this volume has been developed.

Jacqueline Watts

Introduction

Although death, dying and bereavement are universal, they are experienced at an individual level and in a social context with some writers arguing that contemporary beliefs and practices surrounding death and dying are rapidly changing (see, for example, Holloway, 2007). Health and social care practitioners are affected by these changes, which are complex with social, cultural, political, economic, legal and highly personal dimensions. For many people the experience of death and dying is characterised by suffering, engendering feelings of vulnerability, loss of control and uncertainty. The challenges for health and social care practice that aims to respond effectively to this suffering are considerable and in the main derive from two issues. The first is that although modern medicine can prolong life and defer death, the later stages of life are often characterised by incapacity and poor quality of life. The second is linked to the fact that, within the UK National Health Service (NHS), health and social care is a scarce resource with implications for the type and extent of treatment available. Holloway (2007, p. 93) crystallises this issue by asking whether some lives are more valuable than others when it comes to allocating resources or making decisions about treatment. A further question is whether some life-limiting diseases, such as cancer for example, are associated with better levels of care.

The aim of this book, which is set within a UK context, is to provide a knowledge base that contributes to understanding the factors that influence how and where people die, how they and their families are cared for and how, increasingly, death and dying have become the business of a range of professional services. The approach I have taken is to present a range of theoretical perspectives that are thematically organised within each chapter. Drawing on contemporary literatures, these perspectives provide a solid basis from which to consider care practice. In a book this size it is not possible to provide an exhaustive critique of the theoretical and policy debates that currently surround death and dying. The text therefore concentrates on what I judge to be the key issues and offers a scholarly and practical guide suitable for established clinicians, policy makers and managers, as well as for students and those newly involved in the field. The underpinning themes of the book are diversity, communication and palliative care philosophy and practice. These issues are discussed with particular reference to health and social care policy in Scotland, focusing on the recent review of Scottish palliative care services prepared for the Auditor General for Scotland. This report was commissioned in recognition of the likely increased demand for both specialist and general palliative care services in Scotland and also in response to concerns about access across Scotland to well-planned and consistent end of life care.

The book begins with a brief overview of the demographic and social context of death and dying in the UK and considers how death now predominantly occurs in old age, is highly culturally determined and is characterised by a blurring of public and private representations. Death is a common feature of public media in the press, in film and on television but, in private, death is difficult to acknowledge and discuss. Chapters Two and Three discuss the principles and practice of palliative care drawing out details of the holistic model of care that it advocates (Mitchell *et al.*, 2008), and highlighting the critical importance of effective communication on the part of health care practitioners. The focus of Chapter Three is on the hospice movement as institutionalised palliative care practice with particular reference to hospice development in Scotland. The discussion outlines different features of hospice provision including day care, hospice-at-home, in-patient care and its commitment to research and education.

Within the domain of health care, and particularly as part of nursing practice, there has been increasing interest in the importance of understanding and valuing patients' individual spirituality as a function of providing appropriate support for people who are dying. This interest has developed alongside a growing debate among scholars and practitioners about meanings of spirituality, which has become a contested concept particularly in the light of its recent dissociation from religion (Rumbold, 2002). Acknowledging the difficulties this plurality presents to practitioners who support the spiritual needs of dying people (Randall and Downie, 2006; Walter, 2002), Chapter Four considers a range of features that the literature argues now comprise contemporary spirituality (see, for example, Watts, 2008; Watts, 2009d). The implications for practice are discussed in order to provide readers with an understanding of possible approaches to spiritual care based on a differential needs framework.

Death and dying are characterised by loss, and no matter where in the life course a death occurs it may not be easy for those who survive to adjust to the loss. Grief, as both personal and collective expression of loss, is the subject of Chapter Five, which explores grief through a number of theoretical and cultural perspectives. The concepts of anticipatory and disenfranchised grief are considered, as these 'grief types', often overlooked in existing commentaries, can have significant implications for effective and sensitive practice. Examples of unrecognised or disenfranchised grief that may occur, for example in respect of same-sex couples or bereavement through AIDS, are discussed to help practitioners reflect on the different contexts of their practice.

Chapter Six has as its theme the support of bereaved people and draws on different models of practice ranging from the development of support/mutual self-help groups to dedicated professional support from organisations such as Cruse and the Maggie's Centres (first established in Scotland). The work of Walter (1999) informs this chapter, particularly his critique of the various forms of grief counselling that are now a feature of bereavement services across the UK. Included in this chapter is a section devoted to discussion of the particular support needs of bereaved children and young people.

The final chapter brings together the main themes of the book and examines them in the context of policy, focusing mainly on policy initiatives in Scotland. The importance of training and education in skilling professionals, communities and families in their support of dying people is a recurring theme, reminding us that death and dying is everyone's business. The policy emphasis indicates that the care of dying people, particularly among geographically dispersed populations as in many parts of Scotland, will be the responsibility of professionals who, as generalists, will develop skills in end of life care from colleagues who have specialist knowledge in the area. This will facilitate the availability of appropriate high quality 'local' care and obviate the need for dying people to be moved away from their communities to distant specialist care settings.

CHAPTER 1

Death and Dying
in Modern Britain

In the report *Living and Dying Well: a National Action Plan for Palliative and End of Life Care in Scotland* (NHS Scotland, 2008, p. 4) the claim is made that 'patient and family experiences of death and dying are thought to be affected by the lack of familiarity with such concepts and events in our modern society'. The aim of this book is to try and give meaning to these concepts by exploring the ways in which death and dying are negotiated in contemporary society. This opening chapter outlines the demographic and social context of death and dying within the UK, focusing on some of the key features that pertain to Scotland. Issues of cultural and religious diversity are considered together with discussion of the increasingly medicalised approach to death that has become a dominant feature of health care within the UK. The final topic of the chapter is the 'good death', which is explored from both a sociological and cultural perspective.

Life expectancy, cause and setting of death

The past century has seen a significant increase in longevity in Western society due mainly to improved levels of nutrition, health care, education and better quality housing. This has resulted in a marked decline in death registrations in the UK. Leming and Dickinson (2007, p. 15), drawing on a US study into life expectancy conducted in the early 1990s, conclude that science and medicine have increased human life expectancy to its natural limit of around 85 years. In the UK recorded figures indicate that over the past quarter of a century the population has been living longer, but the additional years have not been free from illness or disability. Life expectancy is higher for women than for men; in 2004 the life expectancy at birth for women was 81 years compared to 76.6 years for men (National Statistics Online). The gap in healthy life expectancy between men and women is smaller than for total life expectancy. In 2004, healthy life expectancy at birth was 68 years for men and 70.3 years for women (NSO, 2006). In summary, death in the UK has largely become an event in old age, but with the later years of life characterised by poorer health and/or some form of disability. Longevity has led to an increased expectation that the life span, through medicine, technology and higher living standards, can continue to be stretched (Howarth, 2007). But long life may not be a predictor of quality of life and there has been a rise in the numbers of frail elderly people receiving long-term institutionalised care, living and dying within sequestered communities (Hockey, 1990).

One in four of all people in the UK die from cancer, though cancer is predominantly a disease of the elderly. It is the most common cause of death for men and women aged 50 to 64. Overall, 39% of male and 53% of female deaths in this age group are due to cancer, with lung cancer the most common cause of cancer death for men in this age range. The most common cause of cancer death for women in this age group is breast cancer. For those over the age of 65, circulatory diseases are the most common cause of death, though within this age group, heart disease as a cause of death decreases with age, and strokes increase. Pneumonia as a cause of death also increases with age to account for one in ten deaths among those aged 85 and over (all statistics are taken from NSO, 2006).

The above figures are useful in providing an overview of mortality by disease type but a fuller picture of *how* people die can be gained through information about *where* people die. As Chapters Two and Three will show, the disease type may be a predictor of the setting for death. A survey carried out by Marie Curie in 2004 into the preferred setting for death found that 64% would prefer to die in their own home and 23% in a hospice, with only 4% wanting to die in a hospital (Marie Curie, 2004). Figures for England and Wales for 2005 indicate that 5% of deaths occurred in hospices, 70% in NHS/non-NHS hospitals and just under 20% at home with the remainder in a variety of other institutions and facilities that include psychiatric units and prisons (NSO, 2006). There is a gender variation within these figures with a greater proportion of men dying at home and a slightly smaller proportion of women dying in hospices. Death from natural causes in prison is little discussed and there is a high rate of deaths from infectious diseases in prison in comparison with the population in general.

The picture in Scotland

Scotland has one of the highest rates of mortality in Western Europe and, although rates for the population as a whole have steadily decreased in recent years, deaths among young men in Scotland have been rising with causes related to suicide, alcohol, drugs and violence (Scottish Public Health Observatory, 2008). Over 55,000 people die in Scotland every year with most deaths occurring in those over 65, often following a period of illness and/or frailty (NHS Scotland, 2008). The main causes of death in Scotland follow a pattern similar to that for the UK as a whole. As noted above, life expectancy is increasing but across the UK there are regional disparities. In 2004–6 there was a difference of 12 years in male life expectancy at birth between the lowest and highest areas – the city of Glasgow at 70.5 years and Kensington and Chelsea in London at 83.1 years. As the incidence of cancer increases with age, there are likely to be greater numbers of people living with cancer in the future increasing the requirement for care and support in older age. It is estimated that 36,500 new cases per year will be diagnosed in Scotland by 2020 (SEHD, 2004). Current estimates of the numbers of people who have dementia in Scotland are between 59,000 and 66,000, with these figures expected to rise by 75% by 2031 (SPPC, 2007). Similarly, the number of people with chronic obstructive pulmonary disease in Scotland is predicted to rise by a third in the next twenty years (SPPC, 2007). The effect of these trends on the demand for palliative care services across Scotland is likely to be significant.

In relation to the setting of death, results from a recent Scottish survey indicate that the place of death will be influenced by the cause of death. People dying of cancer are more likely to be supported to die at home or in a hospice (SPPC, 2007). People who died of organ failure were more likely to die in hospital and people with neurological conditions were more likely to die in a care home. Overall, 72% of people died in a hospital or care home (SPPC, 2007), a pattern similar to that for the UK as a whole, although a majority would prefer to die in their own home.

Attitudes towards death and dying

All human beings exist in a social and cultural context and, just as with birth, death is not simply a biological process. Through history death has been imbued with cultural, social and spiritual meaning and this remains so in modern Western society. Attitudes towards death, however, have changed over time and exploring contemporary attitudes towards death and dying is relevant in helping to understand and situate current health and social care approaches to the care of dying people.

Although death is most commonly experienced in old age and therefore may, by some, be regarded as 'timely', it does not follow that death as a universal phenomenon is accepted, talked about or planned for. In the pre-modern period death was experienced as a normal part of life due to poor living conditions, the uncontrolled spread of infectious diseases and high rates of maternal and infant mortality. There existed a widespread social competence in death matters, as this was a community activity and a shared responsibility. Death in modern times is no longer a part of many people's experience and Walter (1992) argues that this lack of 'death experience' contributes to making death taboo and a socially unacceptable topic of conversation. He attributes much of the personal silence around death to the influence of medical discourses that position death as failure and also to the fact that most deaths now occur among older people and are imbued with little social significance, obviating the need for elaborate rites of passage.

The positioning of death as 'forbidden' and 'denied' in modern times has been a key theme in the work of the French historian Phillipe Aries (1981). He cites the influence of the rise of medical practice and the removal of dying to the sanitised space of clinical institutions as pivotal in establishing the silence around death. Walter (2006) explains the contemporary culture of silence about death as a dichotomous one. He argues that death is present in public in relation to its overrepresentation in the media, large-scale catastrophic events and highly publicised homicides, but absent in private, with individuals struggling to make sense of their own mortality and culturally discouraged from talking about loss and grief.

While 'personal' talk of death may be a social embarrassment in contemporary society, its presence in the media, in fine art, theatre, music and in public images of all kinds, is prominent. Violence and death are regularly depicted on film and television programmes and destructive themes, we are told, make for good business (Leming and Dickinson, 2007). These images, however, relate to what is termed 'third person' death, death of others that is beyond our own personal experience. In that sense, fascination and engagement with death that does not have the capacity to touch us personally is safe and non-threatening, because we are telling ourselves that 'it can't happen to me' as a way of denying 'first person' death. This may suggest that we are death denying as individuals but death accepting as a society. Some commentators (for example, Leming and Dickinson, 2007) make the point that people deny death on a personal and individual level because they fear it.

For many, death is something to be avoided for as long as possible and is also something that is feared; this fear is sometimes termed 'death anxiety' (Leming and Dickinson, 2007). Leming and Dickinson (2007) argue that death anxiety is multi-dimensional with fear of dependency, the leaving of loved ones, dying in pain and without dignity, the finality of death and the fate of the material body all potentially significant concerns. They also comment on the issue of whether familiarity with death reduces death anxiety among health care professionals who are routinely confronted with the reality of dying and its consequences. They argue that younger, less-experienced clinicians experience higher levels of death anxiety and are less comfortable with dying patients than longer-serving colleagues. With the development of the hospice movement there has been a gradual opening up of the possibility for both health care professionals and patients to voice these fears, but this is set against a wider cultural background in the West that views death as an extraordinary experience imbued with a sense of mystery and dread.

The influence of religious belief on attitudes to death

The attitudes described above draw on a mainly secular paradigm and do not take account of the different approaches to death of those who hold religious beliefs. While space does not allow for a detailed account of the various religious traditions in respect of the significance of death, it is important to make the point that in many faiths (Christianity, for example) death is seen not as an end but as a transition and so may be welcomed rather than feared or denied. A brief outline of some of the key components of attitudes to death within the main religious traditions is included below to give the reader a sense of the plurality of meanings accorded to death, together with implications for health and social care practice. There is an increasing emphasis on the need for care practice to be culturally sensitive as a way of valuing and respecting the cultural and religious needs of patients (Holloway, 2007). In some institutionalised care settings realising, in a practical way, the preferences of those who are dying may be very difficult.

Within the three main Abrahamic religions (those that recognise a spiritual tradition identified with Abraham), Christianity, Judaism and Islam, monotheism (the belief in one God) is an underpinning belief with life seen as a gift from God that, on death, returns to God. In these three religions a human being is made up of a material body that dies and also of a soul that need not do so. It is the soul that carries the essence of the person and this can remain alive after physical death. This is a unifying concept across these three faiths, which now account for more than half of the world's population. Within these faith traditions, however, there exist different cultural forms and nuances of belief and practice in relation to death and dying.

Within Christian theology multiple traditions have developed. The formal, more ritualised traditions of the Roman Catholic, Anglican and Eastern Orthodox Christian churches place emphasis on death as continuity (Larson-Miller, 2006). Charismatic forms of Protestantism, such as those now widespread both in the UK and the USA, position death as something to be positively anticipated and celebrated (Lucke *et al.*, 2006). These relatively new forms of Protestantism are often community-based and less 'legalistic', in terms of ritual observance, than the long-established churches and represent for many a more informal and personal style of Christian belief.

In Judaism attitudes towards death are shaped by an emphasis on the importance of this earthly lived life, specifically the community expression of faith and the continuity of the Jewish people. The concept of the passage of a dead person's soul to God and to an 'afterlife' was developed by Jewish mystics in the Middle Ages (Golbert, 2006) and, although still present in contemporary Jewish teaching, is not articulated as a central theme. The importance of loved ones accompanying the dying person reflects the Jewish vision of a 'good death' that rejects the idea of dying in a clinical setting among strangers. This powerful desire for a certain type of 'good death' is complicated by the medicalisation and professionalisation of death and dying that 'removes death from the home, the family and the community and from its rightful place in the life cycle' (Golbert, 2006, p. 53).

The significance of life after death is a fundamental tenet of Islam with rewards or punishments in the next life determined both by the strength of a person's faith and by the moral quality of their earthly life. The polarities of hell and paradise are important elements of Islamic teaching concerning the 'next life' with hell characterised as a place of torment for unbelievers and wrongdoers and paradise depicted as a place of beauty and youthful health where there is no trace of sickness, pain or old age (Campo, 2006). This physical and spiritual paradise, as Islamic heaven, comprises numerous levels, with the higher levels reserved as a reward to those who have been more virtuous. Islamic texts teach that all those admitted to paradise will remain there for eternity. Within Islam death is seen as divinely ordained and thus to be accepted. Campo (2006, p. 154), however, makes the point that death beliefs and practices are subject to 'different Islamic religious traditions, ethnicities, nationalities and sensibilities' and, therefore, cannot be seen as homogeneous.

Among the eastern non-Abrahamic faiths such as Buddhism and Hinduism, teaching about death has developed to embrace the cultural traditions of countries to which they have spread, such as India, Thailand, Tibet and Japan. Goss and Klass (2006, p. 69) argue that within Buddhism 'death is the fundamental transition in human life'. They also make the point that a perception of all things as impermanent forms the basis of Buddhist teaching, with mindfulness as the essence of the Buddhist approach to confronting death, which is viewed as a real and inevitable part of life. In this tradition both life and death are integral to the path of enlightenment. Also integral to the Buddhist approach to death is belief in karma, which Goss and Klass (2006, p. 72) characterise as 'the law of cause and effect', meaning that right actions have good effects and bad actions have bad effects; the accumulation of good deeds leads to a better rebirth.

Hindu approaches to death are shaped by an understanding that the dead have an ongoing influence on the living and, because of this, death is not feared but accepted. This acceptance is karma and is a fundamental state of being for Hindus. For those Hindus living in the diaspora in the West, although the precept of karma may be unchanged from its lived reality in the Indian sub-continent (the original cultural home of Hinduism), the practices associated with the requirement to be culturally and ritually 'with' the dying person are often difficult to apply. Elmore (2006) cites, for example, the constraints of Western medicalised settings that do not allow patients to die on the earth, as Hindu tradition requires, and prevent relatives from sitting with the deceased singing religious texts. These constraints may cause spiritual distress and have had the effect of Hindu communities invoking different forms of ritual compromise to negotiate the space between the traditional origins of Hinduism and the new cultures within which many Hindus now live (Elmore, 2006; Firth, 2000). Sikhism, which in relation to some of its rituals and practices connected to death and dying has some similarity with Hinduism, also has had to reconsider which elements from its main tradition can be adapted to other contexts beyond those of its origins (Myrvold, 2006).

Management of death and dying

As discussed above, death and dying in the UK have changed significantly over the past century with very different patterns of dying emerging. This has been due, in no small part, to the establishment of the NHS, bringing with it expectations that medicine would sooner or later find a cure for all conditions, with death seen as a failure of medical staff and the institutions they serve. The emphasis on medical research and practice within the NHS has been heavily oriented towards cure with the development of sophisticated technology and drug interventions increasingly able to keep death at bay, but with ultimate cures for diseases such as cancer and heart disease remaining elusive. The highly medicalised and science-driven setting of UK hospitals has contributed to the disciplining of death against a background of multiple treatment options that can result in inhumane suffering and indignity at the hands of clinicians. Issues of control, choice and what might be conceptualised as the shadowy space between life and death have become matters of concern. Kaufman (2005) provides fascinating insight into what, within the acute hospital setting, it means to be not fully alive but not quite dead, especially for those dying in old age.

Frank (1995, p. 111), in considering these issues, draws on his three-dimensional model of illness narratives; these are categorised as chaos, restitution and quest narratives. He describes the chaos narrative that points to loss of hope and eventual death as one that cannot be entertained by clinicians because 'chaos is an implicit critique of the modernist assumptions of clinical work'. Restitution narratives reflect the patient as 'better now', while quest narratives are reconstructive in nature, drawing new resources from the illness experience to enhance quality of life. There is great insight in Frank's (1995) critique of what death represents to many in medical practice, and he makes a powerful argument that continuing to extend life at any cost may have the unintended effect of eroding the quality of life. The language of medicine and technical possibilities have colonised this debate with the consequence that dying of old age, or being simply worn out, are no longer acknowledged options. As research and technology continue to drive the development of new treatments and techniques, one consequence is that some people may find themselves on an almost endless dying continuum, lingering without capacity but not allowed to die. For many, dying has become more feared than death itself (Kellehear, 1984).

As part of the increased management of death and dying, there has been a growth in the professionalisation of a range of associated services from undertaking to bereavement support, all contributing to an expanding 'death industry'. Jupp and Walter (1999) cite as an example of this trend towards professionalisation and commercialisation the change in image undertakers have conferred upon their businesses in recent times, now referring to themselves as funeral directors. Such businesses offer a full package of services with many having private mortuaries and 'chapels of rest' (Jupp and Walter, 1999). It is thus no longer necessary for families to keep the body of a deceased family member at home in the days leading up to the funeral, as once was customary within traditional Christian practice. The professional and individualised service provided by crematoria (this now being the most popular method of disposal) to create a personal 'customer-led' funeral is another example of the way in which expertise in specific areas of death and dying have been appropriated by professional specialists. Although over the past quarter of a century there has been a significant decline in the number of burials, this period has seen a rise in a new breed of professional cemetery staff who, increasingly supported by academic researchers, have been interested in considering different environmental burial options ('green' funerals are one example) and ways of making best use of existing land (Jupp and Walter, 1999). Where bereavement support is concerned, increasingly this is now the province of professionally trained counsellors and therapists (Bryant-Jefferies, 2006), many of whom work within the voluntary sector. In former times this kind of support was a community activity, not professionally organised but 'organically' provided. We see the continuation of this kind of community support mainly within faith groups, with care of the bereaved framed by prescribed mourning rituals and practices.

Dying today has become a behind-the-scenes activity delegated to the safe domain of health care professionals. With chronic illness and the frailty of old age failing to provide a definitive 'death-bed scene for ourselves or our families' (Kellehear, 2007, p. 213), death now is seen to require 'managing'. Community and family participation in caring for dying people has been replaced by 'expert' skilled care. It is this area of the day-to-day care of dying people, now the concern of a wide range of health care organisations including hospices, that has seen the biggest growth in professionalisation. The development and organisation of hospices is the theme of Chapter Three but, drawing on hospice discourses of professionalism, it is relevant here to briefly make links to its approach to dealing with the 'physical reality of deferred death' discussed above (Jupp and Walter, 1999, p. 272). This approach is predicated on palliative care principles that are the subject of the next chapter; these now frame specialist education and practice in caring for dying people with advanced disease who may have been dying for a long time but whose condition has been managed by drug and other therapies. A controlled, pain-free death that involves patients being 'accompanied' by skilled professionals has come to be seen as the new 'good death' (see below).

The rise of professionalisation in all the different domains of death and dying has not been without its critics, some of whom (for example, Kellehear,

2005) question the value to communities of professional helpers and 'experts' whose efforts may serve to de-skill individuals and communities in supporting dying people.

Quality of dying – the 'good death'

The concept of a 'good death' is highly contested and definitions vary according to different historical periods and cultural contexts. Kellehear (2007, p. 90) cites two commonly used derivatives of the term: the first draws on the Greek words *eu thanatos* (closely associated to the English euthanasia) meaning a death that is swift and painless and morally correct. The second derivative refers to the Greek *kalos thanatos* which means a beautiful death but with the added characteristic of preparedness. This form of 'good death' is not sudden but imbued with foresight and significant social meaning.

In contemporary Britain the formerly powerful religious precepts of the Church in respect of the proper conduct of death and dying has given way to a plurality of preferred death behaviours among its culturally diverse population. The rise of secularism and individualism has resulted in the 'authority of the self' (Walter, 1994, p. 27) with almost limitless personal choice as the new prescription. The idea of an all-embracing definition of a 'good death' that would be meaningful to even a sizeable proportion of Britain's population seems beyond reasonable expectation. Instead, there exists a complex web of the social, the cultural and the personal that blends to produce individualised understandings of what contributes to a 'good death'. For many, this relates to living a good life (Sandman, 2005, p. 7).

A gradual rejection of a single prescribed system of beliefs has taken hold in contemporary Britain, which has become a multi-cultural and multi-faith society, particularly in densely populated urban areas where mosques, synagogues and Hindu temples are to be found alongside churches representing a range of Christian denominations. A wide range of death practices and rituals are now part of Britain's 'death landscape' but, for some, these are enacted against a backdrop of cultural constraint caused by standardised systems at the centre of institutionalised environments. For example, Firth (2001) critiques the ways in which British Hindus, in the light of the increasing professionalisation of death in the UK, have had to adapt their rituals to preserve the essential 'ingredients' of a good Hindu death. She argues that for many immigrant communities creative compromise is needed to maintain the integrity of dying in a way that is sacred and meaningful both to the dying person and their family. With much media coverage devoted to faith issues (often framed by the language of difference) it is, however, easy to overlook the increasing secularisation of UK society, particularly in relation to death practices (Walter, 1994).

Because of the contested meaning of the term 'good death', with its contextual variables (for example, place of death, timeliness, religious rituals and preparedness), Bradbury's (2000) conceptual framework is useful in establishing three broad categories of 'ideal' good deaths. Her model of the sacred, medical and natural 'good death' identifies three different 'types' of dying. The model incorporates elements of Kellehear's (2007) dual derivative of the term discussed above to illustrate the dynamic and negotiated meaning of the concept. The sacred death is associated with religious faith, particularly belief in an afterlife with death as a stage or transition and often a cause for celebration. Although the details vary across different religions, a key component of the sacred death is the quality of life lived by the deceased (with an emphasis on good works and a moral code) and the manner and setting of their death, with the dying person remaining conscious until the point of death an important feature. This type of traditional 'good death' is a shared experience and is often associated with pre-industrial and/or non-Western societies, with images of the family in attendance at the deathbed very common. In contrast, the medical 'good death' is now an established feature of mature societies. It embraces medical techniques that offer opportunities to manage dying by, for example, deferring death with the use of sophisticated technologies. The easing of pain through the use of drugs is a medical procedure that has shifted control over the experience of dying from the dying person to the professional (Bradbury, 2000, p. 61).

In modern Britain this control is often enacted in the setting of the hospital or hospice and is associated with increasing professionalisation of end-of-life care, which has had the effect of making dying more impersonal. The role of the 'expert' is one feature of the medicalised 'good death' in contemporary Britain. The natural 'good death', Bradbury (2000) argues, has been subject to some re-invention and flexible characterisation with two principal variations. The first involves the active and informed participation of the dying person in their treatment, often rejecting what may be seen as harmful and unnecessary medical interventions. In this sense this can be understood as a 'less-medicalised good death'. The second natural 'good death' relates to sudden and unexpected death occurring often in an everyday setting – during a leisure pursuit, for example, or dying of a heart attack at work. These deaths are quick, painless and free of medical intervention (Bradbury, 1996, p. 90).

However, they may not be pain-free for the bereaved and, in some cases, can lead to complicated grief reactions with the consequent use of one or more forms of 'organised' bereavement care and support (Walter, 1999).

Walter's (1999) observation raises the important point that the various definitions and dimensions of a 'good death' discussed above do not address the critical question of good for whom. A more fundamental question is whether a death can ever be good. In terms of the issue of 'good for whom', features that affect the perception of the quality of death include the dimensions of age, timeliness, the needs and preferences of the dying person, their readiness for death, their suffering and the setting of death. Elsewhere I have written, for example, about the devastating impact on me of the sudden and totally unexpected death of my father at the age of 63 from a heart attack (Watts, 2009a). The shock of his death and the resulting overwhelming anguish and grief shaped my life for many years. Not being able to share his later years of retirement or say goodbye and thank you has been a constant source of sadness and regret and it is only in more recent years that I have been able to critically reflect that his death, without pain or suffering, might be considered a 'good death' for him even though 'bad' for me at the time. The contrast of his quick death with, for example, the lingering social death of many Alzheimer's sufferers, in advance of their biological death and the ongoing losses experienced by them and their families, serves as a reminder that quality as well as quantity of life is a significant factor in any discussion of quality of death.

The sociologist Weisman (1972) incorporates this dimension within his concept of 'appropriate death', which some commentators see as a preferred alternative to the dichotomous paradigm of 'good' and 'bad' death. In his critique of 'appropriate death' Weisman (1972) argues that there are four principal requirements: conflict is reduced, compatibility with the ego or true self is achieved, continuity of important relationships is preserved or restored and, lastly, that consummation of a wish is brought about. An underpinning theme of this model is that death should be consistent with the aims and values we have followed through life. In the case of someone who dies while undertaking a sporting activity such as sky-diving, for example, their death might be seen as one consistent with their sense of adventure and risk-taking. Sandman (2005, p. 27), however, commenting on this model, makes the point that 'the whole idea about consistency seems to rest on the idea that we have well established and well defined self-identities, which should influence the way we die – something that might not be true'. Sandman's (2005) critique includes the dimension of a dignified death. He argues that this has become synonymous with 'good' in the literature and is centred on a valuing of the person and their wishes that confers integrity, with being able to remain a person and continue to live until the moment of death an important component of that integrity.

The discussion has considered a number of features that affect the quality of dying, particularly some general characteristics from the literature about what can contribute to different types of 'good death' within a pluralist society such as we have in the UK. Bradbury's (2000) conceptual framework has been widely used to inform understanding of how end-of-life care practice can support individuals to have the death they want. Although Bradbury's (2000) three categories of 'good death' have distinct features, in practice they may often overlap to reveal complex social representations of both 'good' and 'bad' dying that produce highly individualised perspectives of what it means to die well. Bradbury's (2000) model suggests that a death can only be judged 'good' in relation to specific criteria and this will depend on which criteria are utilised. The reality of most deaths in contemporary Britain is that, in these theoretical terms, they are a mix of more than one of these forms, with many overseen by clinicians in their attempts to manage and control the dying process. In some quarters, clinicians are seen as having a central role in making a good death possible. Murray and Sheikh (2008, p. 959) go further, arguing that 'facilitating a good death should be recognised as a core clinical proficiency, as basic as diagnosis and treatment'.

The challenge for policy of incorporating a 'good death' competence (Murray and Sheikh, 2008) within clinical medicine has been taken up by the recently established specialty of palliative medicine, which has gradually become incorporated within many general hospitals as well as within hospices and dedicated palliative care units. The importance of psychosocial, spiritual and cultural, as well as clinical, components of a 'good death' is acknowledged within hospice and palliative care philosophy and practice and, increasingly, informs policy development in end-of-life care. This philosophy, that aims to 'get end of life care right' (Murray and Sheikh, 2008, p. 958), has a well-developed body of theory but does not easily lend itself to objective evaluation. These and other related concerns form the key themes of the next two chapters.

CHAPTER 2

Palliative Care Philosophy and Practice

In the public mind palliative care and the care setting called a hospice are inextricably linked. In recent years, however, palliative care as a clinical specialty has become established within many general hospitals and is now widely practised beyond hospices in a range of community contexts. Holloway (2007, p. 96) develops this point, claiming that 'extension of its philosophy and practice into all healthcare settings is currently the main thrust of palliative care'. This chapter is devoted to a discussion of palliative care, both as theory and practice, while Chapter Three charts the development of the hospice movement (the original institutional base of palliative care) and considers some of the challenges it currently faces.

Palliative care is a relatively new health care discipline that originated as a response to the inadequate provision of mainstream services for the dying. The resulting development of the hospice movement, which is predicated on palliative care philosophy (see below), has seen a burgeoning of hospice provision across the UK, with many hospices now partly or wholly absorbed within the National Health Service (Clark and Seymour, 1999). Most palliative care organisations have as a basic aim the support of dying people and their families. This is achieved through a range of services and interventions that include care in the community, day care, in-patient units where patients can have symptom relief, bereavement groups and education forums. The increasing medicalisation of palliative care, with its adherence to 'routinized' practices (James and Field, 1992), is now well documented, as is its gradual mainstreaming within healthcare services that are highly bureaucratic, professionalised, audit bound and evidence-based (Woods, 2007). Despite this trend towards absorption within mainstream medicine, palliative care has gained almost universal social approval and its social responsibility for the dying is highly valued (Sinclair, 2007).

What is palliative care?

The concept of palliative care is multi-dimensional and there are a number of definitions in the literature each with its particular nuances. The definition of palliative care given by the World Health Organisation (WHO) is as follows:

> Palliative care is an approach that improves the quality of life of patients and their families facing the problems associated with life-threatening illness, through the prevention and relief of suffering by means of early identification and impeccable assessment and treatment of pain and other problems, physical, psychosocial and spiritual. (WHO, 2002)

This WHO definition is underpinned by the philosophy of palliative care, which embraces multi-disciplinarity, affirms life and accepts death as a normal process, intends neither to hasten nor postpone death and sees the application of palliative care principles as relevant early in the course of illness. Palliative care is, therefore, not just concerned with care in the last days or weeks of a person's life, but has relevance at every stage of the disease process from diagnosis onwards. In general terms, palliative care can be understood as inter-professional co-ordinated care of the whole person when curative treatment is no longer possible. The concept of 'total pain', as a central tenet of palliative care practice, is based on the way in which a dying person's symptoms impact on their physical, emotional, social, spiritual and psychological wellbeing, with the goal of palliative care being achievement of the best quality of life for patients and their families within the constraints of a life-limiting illness. This care also extends to patients' family and friends, and Randall and Downie (2006, p. 75) note that this 'belief in obligations to relatives is rarely questioned in palliative care'. They argue that this potentially may involve ethical dilemmas for the health care team with, for example, the interests of patient confidentiality compromised by assumed responsibilities to the family. The balance between making the patient comfortable and keeping the family comfortable may thus come into play here. They make the further related point that the emphasis on family-centred care may not take account of conflicts of interest that may arise between patient and family. Both policy and practice cannot thus be applied in a standardised way but should consider each patient in his or her family context.

Twycross (2003) offers a more developed framework of what constitutes palliative care, identifying further features as person- rather than disease-focused, death accepting and life enhancing, a partnership approach between patient and carers, and concerned with healing rather than cure. Where cure is not possible the concept of healing becomes contested and, for some, meaningless. Twycross (2003), however, associates healing with relationships and, as outlined in the previous chapter, Weisman (1972) argues that the preservation or restoration of relationships is central to what he terms an 'appropriate death' that incorporates emotional healing. Palliative care philosophy acknowledges that this emotional healing requires multi-disciplinary input and has a commitment to a partnership approach in the form of inter-professional team-working in recognition of the complex social and practical needs of dying people and their families. Drawing on the skills of social workers, complementary therapists and counsellors as well as doctors and nurses to provide seamless support, it comprises a holistic service with an appropriate spread of expertise. The reality, particularly in relation to hospital palliative care teams, is that co-ordination of input across professional boundaries is complex and labour-intensive and subject to differing professional hierarchies and understandings (Clark and Seymour, 1999). In one example I recently came across a patient who, having undergone extensive surgery for throat cancer, received a visit at his home from a social worker before he had been discharged from hospital. The purpose of the visit was to identify his support needs on returning home. The inter-professional communication had somewhere broken down, leaving the patient less than confident that the palliative care team knew what they were doing.

In institutionalised settings nurses are the main palliative caregivers, and Payne and Seymour (2004), writing for the nursing community, add further insight into contemporary meanings of palliative care. Their framework acknowledges dying as a normal process, advocates multi-disciplinary team working in the care of patients to enable them to live as actively as possible until the point of death, and sees palliative care as relevant early in the course of illness rather than as simply an end-stage clinical support. At the core of these definitions is the philosophy of holistic care of the dying person contributing to the continually evolving ideology of the good death as a sequel to a life lived to the end (Clark and Seymour, 1999). Chapter One explored contemporary meanings of a good death, the idea of which was shown to vary over time and be a function of tradition, faith and culture (Seale, 1998). The close association of palliative care with the good death is now firmly established but some would argue (see Lawton, 2000, for example) that this has essentially become little more than a mantra as part of a reductionist approach to the management of dying that focuses primarily on symptom control. Indeed, Payne and Seymour (2004, p. 4) foreground this debate asking 'is palliative care about dying or symptom control?'

Palliative care philosophy has bereavement care as part of its remit (Cobb, 2004) with a stated commitment to support families, as well as patients, both before and after death. There has been an increased emphasis on this element and now bereavement support is offered within the hospice setting, within general hospitals and within the community (provided by community nurses) (Birtwistle, 2004). Palliative care practitioners are trained in this area of support and work in partnership with other bereavement workers and professional counsellors. Bereavement support is provided in different ways but often will continue for the first year of bereavement as a way of acknowledging particular landmarks in the grief trajectory.

As an area of developing specialist health and social care practice, palliative care is committed to an ongoing programme of research and education in end-of-life care specifically to enhance understanding of the ways in which practitioners can help patients to both 'live and die well'. These activities can be conceptually merged as a form of scholarship that Sneddon (2004) characterises as a process undertaken *with* and *for* people, distinguishing this from a traditional sociological research paradigm where research is conducted *on* people. Kellehear (2008, p. 145) characterises the '*with*' and '*for*' mode as 'participatory relations' where equal relations are based on mutual interests that recognise the different types and levels of expertise that partners bring to the research encounter. This emancipatory approach runs counter to the traditional research and teaching hierarchies that are present in most medical and nurse education programmes. Emphasis on research and education, as a key component of palliative care philosophy, is sometimes lost amidst the dominant clinical practice discourses of drug interventions, symptom control and pain management, and it is only in very recent times that we have begun to see the emergence of a broader palliative care literature that draws on wider sociological, cultural and philosophical traditions. Much of this literature emphasises psychosocial aspects, which MacLeod (2008) argues often present as particularly difficult areas of practice; some of these issues are outlined later in this chapter.

Acknowledging loss

At the core of palliative care philosophy is an 'opening up' of dying (Holloway, 2007, p. 95) which acknowledges that suffering has many dimensions and meanings in the lives of the terminally ill (Salt, 1997). Within this frame attention is directed to the 'small' as well as the 'large' losses that can negatively impact on quality of life. A brief discussion of some of these losses identified in the literature has particular relevance for practice and will reveal the importance of support that starts from where the patient is (see below). Referring to the family context, Altschuler (2005) documents how, for example, in the case of a parent of young children, there can be a gradual loss of role and withdrawal from parenting activities as the illness progresses. She also highlights how deteriorating health can render parents emotionally unavailable to their children. Armstrong-Coster (2004) develops the ways in which uncertainty and loss of control in the lives of those suffering from advanced cancer can challenge how they see themselves, with increasing dependence on others leading to the re-negotiation of relationships. The issues of appearance and the way one 'is seen' are also significant losses for many cancer patients as hair and weight loss (and sometimes weight gain) can contribute to a sense of disfigurement (Lawton, 2000; Armstrong-Coster, 2004).

The further losses of the 'social self' (Cassell, 1991) and income-earning capacity have been discussed by DeSpelder and Strickland (2005), who note how these losses may result in a decreasing sense of self-worth. Life-threatening illness disrupts virtually all aspects of a person's life and space here does not allow for an in-depth discussion of these, except to note that palliative care acknowledges that these may be cumulative and contribute to what can be understood as a 'trajectory of suffering', conceptualised by Salt (1997, p. 58) as 'a complex state of being'.

Palliative care in practice

So far this chapter has explored some of the key principles of palliative care philosophy and has begun to consider some of the implications for practice. It is important to recognise that issues for practice, particularly professional practice, will vary according to the type of practice (for example, social work, medicine or nursing), the setting and the context. Multi-professional team working that operates across organisational boundaries is at the core of palliative care. A dying person and their family may receive care and support from a plethora of individuals, including the GP, district nurse, health visitor, Macmillan nurse, social worker, physiotherapist, spiritual adviser, dietician, bereavement worker, home carer and specialist palliative care nurse. Most 'hands-on' palliative care in the community is undertaken by the district nurse, with guidance from the specialist palliative care nurse often prompted by a change in the patient's condition.

Who leads and co-ordinates the team can be a contentious matter: this may not be a function of seniority and can vary according to the skills and knowledge of individual team members. What is important is that all aspects of care are co-ordinated in response to the needs and problems of the dying person. As an example from my own experience, a friend dying from lung cancer, with only days to live, wanted to go shopping to buy a watch as a birthday present for his young son. During a visit by the social worker to him at home where he was receiving care, he asked her for the use of a wheelchair to make the shopping trip possible. She refused to arrange this on the grounds that he was too weak. He telephoned his specialist palliative care nurse to ask again for the loan of a wheelchair, which she subsequently arranged. My friend made that special purchase and was able to give the gift that he had chosen to his son. He died early the following day. In that instance it was the specialist nurse who had taken the decision to respond positively to the request, understanding the importance to my friend of being able to undertake the shopping expedition and of what it might mean to his son.

Palliative care can be understood as a set of skills; at the most general level these include the skills of active listening, goal setting, decision making, crisis intervention, advocacy and bereavement counselling, all of which require the key skill of interpersonal communication. In the case of nurses and doctors further clinical skills related to treatment regimes and pain management are learned and refined in the practice setting. Because communication is seen as central to palliative care practice (Frank, 2004) this topic comprises the theme of the discussion below, which introduces a theoretical model of awareness contexts to help explore why effective communication with dying people and their families can be difficult. Communicating with patients and their families is informed by ethical considerations and the discussion will consider some key ethical precepts in health care. In order to situate this discussion it is important to briefly explore the range of settings for palliative care practice.

Hospices are the main setting and base for specialist palliative care practice and the organisational and cultural development of this movement is discussed in Chapter Three. I use the term 'base' in respect of hospices as much care undertaken under their guidance now takes place, not in institutional clinical environments, but in the community, often in the homes of dying people. The now familiar 'Hospice at Home' service run by charities such as Marie Curie and Macmillan is one example. Under this model specially trained doctors and nurses give medical and nursing care in a way similar to in-patient hospice services. Many general hospitals have established palliative care teams to oversee the end-stage illness of dying patients and provide specialist advice and support to the generalist nursing and medical staff, who may have received little training in caring for dying people. Higginson *et al.* (2002), in their review of palliative care provision in hospital, hospice and home, found that one of the most consistent effects of palliative care in all these settings was improved satisfaction for carers and to a lesser extent for patients when compared with conventional or non-hospice services. They also found that there appears to be an advantage of multi-disciplinary over uni-disciplinary teams.

As will be discussed below, some writers argue that among those most in need of palliative care are the large numbers of very old people who receive long-term residential care. In these settings we are seeing a gradual, but slow, move towards the implementation of the palliative approach, which seeks to enhance quality rather than longevity of life, emphasising psychosocial and spiritual aspects as well as the purely physical. Katz (2001), however, has argued that this focus on enhancing quality of life is at the expense of emphasis on quality of dying. Some providers of social housing, however, have begun to offer 'extra care housing' to support the end-of-life care needs of their residents. The housing association Housing 21, for example, has initiated projects in north-east England and East Anglia with 24-hour care and support services to enable terminally ill extra-care tenants to die in their own home if that is their wish (Housing 21 website).

Communication

The issue of communication within palliative care practice is an inter-professional concern for nurses, doctors and social workers alike. It is a key component of psychosocial and spiritual care, both important elements of support for people with a terminal diagnosis. Communication has verbal and non-verbal components and issues of language, setting and style are all relevant. In short, communication is a huge topic and many texts and manuals have been written about different modes, techniques and approaches in a range of contexts. For the current purpose I will concentrate on some key elements of communication behaviours to offer a critical perspective on issues for professional practice in end-of-life care.

In the health care encounter the significance of communication begins with the presentation of symptoms, attendance for exploratory tests, diagnosis and the consequent discussion about treatment options; it then continues throughout the experience of illness. While there are different types of communication, it is the form that Frank (2004) terms dialogue, a two-way exchange, that will be the focus of the discussion that follows. Frank (2004) argues that dialogue is central to the face-to-face encounter between patient and health care professional and that often this is not a satisfactory exchange, either for the patient or for the health professional. Randall and Downie (2006) support this view, suggesting that one reason for this reported poor quality interaction might be communication skills training for health care workers. They argue that this training may inhibit rather than enhance authenticity so that intuitive, genuine reactions to patients' stories and questions are replaced by trained responses that may obviate the need for the health professional to give the patient their whole attention. Such artificial responses could also be attributed to strategies of avoidance whereby carers confine themselves to instrumental communication and the performing of mechanical tasks as a way of avoiding the emotional encounter because it is too painful. This can be understood as a protection mechanism on the part of the carer and is referred to in the literature as 'distancing' (Buckman, 2000). Because, as Frank (2004, p. 111) explains, 'palliative care seeks to prevent the absolute death – being unheard, unrecognised and unremembered', unsatisfactory communication, of the type described by Randall and Downie (2006), is particularly problematic within end-of-life care, where the issues of disclosure and truth telling, both complex processes, are ongoing. There is no doubt that this is a difficult area and one practical suggestion made by Randall and Downie (2006) is that health workers should provide only the information that patients indicate they want and in language that they find meaningful.

Kellehear (2008, p. 148) contends that being diagnosed with a life-threatening illness such as HIV or cancer is a kin to being 'hit by a bomb', such is the devastating impact of receiving this diagnosis. This breaking of bad news has been the subject of extensive critique in the literature with discussion of different communication techniques and follow-up strategies of dominant interest. Whatever approach is taken, the delivery of this news is a critical disclosure. It is always challenging for the health professional and is often difficult to 'receive' by the patient. Disclosure is a process of providing information that involves 'telling' (though not necessarily all at once) and stages for 'retelling', reflection, clarification and discussing and interpreting information. By the time patients are referred for palliative care they will usually be aware of their diagnosis and some will be experiencing deteriorating health as 'temporary survivors'. The challenge for palliative care practitioners in their communication with patients is to maintain channels of openness so that patients and their families can discuss their concerns and uncertainties. Some of these may include questions such as 'can I be cured?', 'how long have I got?' and 'will I die in pain?'. Responding to these types of questions can be ethically and emotionally challenging for health care workers who find themselves in a relationship with patients, helping them to adjust to changed realities. What dying people know or don't know or want to acknowledge about their situation influences the ways in which all others interact with them, framing the cognitive limit of clinician/patient interaction.

The trend towards 'openness' in all areas of health care communication is a fairly recent phenomenon and our understanding of how openness or lack of it operates in health care practice has been drawn mainly from the work of Glaser and Strauss (1965) and their 'awareness contexts' model with its four dimensions that correspond to the levels of knowledge that dying patients have:

- open awareness where both the dying person and the health-care professional know what is wrong and the likely prognosis and acknowledge this to each other;
- suspected awareness where the dying person suspects what is wrong but does not communicate this to the health carer;
- mutual pretence awareness where both the dying patient and the health care professional know what is wrong but do not acknowledge this to each other;
- closed awareness where the dying person does not know what is wrong and is unaware of the prognosis and the health-care professional does know.

In the early part of the twenty-first century it is likely that patients will be informed directly by specialist doctors that they have a life-limiting condition, with family practitioners (GPs) often involved in re-stating the diagnosis (Seamark *et al.*, 2008). This initial breaking of bad news may confirm what is already suspected by the patient, but whether or not this is the case there should be an opportunity to then review what information the patient already has or would like. Buckman (2000) identifies this 'starting from where the patient is' as a pre-eminent principle of any act of caring and it is this principle that has been advocated as a central tenet of sensitive and effective communication within palliative care. This he argues can be achieved by sensitivity to non-verbal as well as verbal cues and by the building of trust through making the person feel special.

Although open awareness is now the most common of Glaser and Strauss's (1965) categories, this has a number of elements that have challenges for practice, most of which will have an ethical dimension. In relation to this, Field and Copp (1999) argue that palliative care's ideological commitment to open awareness has shifted to conditional openness, partially because, although physicians may be forthcoming in disclosing the original diagnosis, they may be less forthcoming about disclosing terminal prognosis. Furthermore, it may not be appropriate to assume that an open awareness model can be utilised for all dying people and sensitivity on the part of health-care workers to the cultural and individual needs of patients is key to good practice. Howarth (2007) makes the further point that the open awareness model may be more difficult to apply in settings other than the hospice, where patients are fully aware of the terminal status of their illness.

Ethical principles

Most aspects of health care raise moral problems that make it difficult for professional practitioners to make best interest judgements on behalf of their patients as part of their professional duty to do good (Ellershaw and Garrard, 2004). Within health care there exists an abundance of duties, with a duty of care to patients on the part of clinicians seen as an overriding duty. The concept of a duty of care is multi-faceted and the ethicists Beauchamp and Childress (2001) suggest that there are four moral principles that capture the core of ethical practice within the domain of health care and are central components of a clinician's duty of care to patients. These principles, often referred to in the literature as 'the four principles', are beneficence, non-maleficence, respect for autonomy, and justice, and are widely seen as applicable within broad health and social care practice.

These principles are not absolute, exceptionless principles and neither do they operate in isolation; each is constrained by one or more of the others. Of these no single principle is always the most important and which one is prioritised will depend on the particular features and context of each individual case. They do not offer a formula for decision-making and neither do they remove the need for sensitive moral judgement. They do, however, provide a general moral guide about how to act, though it is the particular circumstances of each situation that will determine right actions.

1 *Beneficence* tells us to do good to the patient and to act in a way that will benefit the patient and contribute positively to their health

and welfare. The imperative to do good means that the patient must consider that the outcome of the action is good. The emphasis here is that the action is for the good of the patient (not self). Being sure that the action is 'good' requires the practitioner to be clear about what the patient wants, particularly in light of the inherently subjective nature of individual welfare (Molyneux, 2007).

2. *Non-maleficence* tells us to do the patient no harm. The implications of this are we should not cause pain or suffering and neither should we injure or incapacitate the patient. In health care, even if little or no good can be done, there is a primary duty to avoid harming the patient (Mason and Whitehead, 2003).

3. *Respect for autonomy* tells us to respect the wishes, choices and preferences of the patient (Kinlaw, 2005). Autonomy is characterised by the capacity for self-rule, to think and make decisions independently without coercion or manipulation by others. Autonomous decisions are ones taken by competent agents who have been fully informed about their situation outside the controlling influence of others, with this central to informed consent. Implications of this are that, for patients to make informed decisions, they must be told the truth about their condition, and privacy and confidentiality should be maintained so that unwanted controlling interventions by others (possibly friends or family members) are avoided. Randall and Downie (2000) further conceptualise autonomy as a critical feature of the patients' rights movement that itself has developed as part of a general democratisation of modern society.

4. *Justice* tells us to treat people fairly, which involves ensuring that the costs and benefits of treatment are fairly distributed between patients. This also entails paying attention to the appropriateness of treatments that includes a risk/benefits approach to complement the costs/benefits approach that has implications both for the individual and management of limited resources (Woods, 2007, p. 79).

Within health and social care respect for autonomy and dignity has come to be seen as central to patient- or client-centredness, particularly within the philosophy and practice of palliative care (Randall and Downie, 2006). Some narratives (see Mason and Whitehead, 2003) suggest that the moral principle of autonomy is increasingly being afforded primacy by health-care professionals, especially by palliative care practitioners. The concept of autonomy is linked to respect for someone else's autonomy; respect for our own autonomy is important to us and respect for the autonomy of others flows from this. These issues are often complex with practitioners required to balance a number of ethical considerations; some case study examples follow to illustrate this complexity.

James is an 80-year-old man suffering from terminal cancer. He has been admitted to a hospice but is anxious to go home; he lives alone with no family nearby and no social support. At the hospice, a nurse who has got to know him well recognises how important it is for James to go home to die and, in respecting his autonomy, begins to make the appropriate plans. These are subsequently overruled by a senior member of the hospice staff who considers James to be at risk of harm by going home where, in his frail state, she believes that he will be unable to undertake any of the usual daily living tasks of washing, shopping, cooking, etc as he requires round-the-clock nursing. He has expressed a desire to go home to be alone and has declined the offer of home support. The ethical principles of *beneficence*, *non-maleficence* and *respect for autonomy* are all relevant, though in conflict. From the health professional's point of view the duty to do no harm may be pre-eminent but this has to be weighed against respecting James's wishes and it could be argued that, because his wish is so strong, enabling James to return home will be an act of beneficence because it will contribute positively to his well-being as he defines it.

A second case study concerns Rachel who has been suffering from multiple sclerosis for many years. She is in her early sixties and has been widowed some years earlier. She lives near her married daughter and enjoys family life. She has become increasingly incapacitated and her GP has recommended that she be admitted to the local hospice as her condition has begun to deteriorate rapidly. Rachel is Jewish and is concerned that she may not be able to have her Kosher food. Rachel's daughter is also worried that the hospice staff may tell Rachel of her impending death; she is adamant that should this happen Rachel would give up hope for the life that remains. She explains that maintaining hope is a central belief within Judaism. This situation relates to truth telling and poses an ethical dilemma. If Rachel asks a nurse if she is dying what should the nurse do? If respecting Rachel's autonomy, expressed by Rachel to her daughter as not wanting to be told that she is dying, means the nurse has to withhold the truth or even lie, is this ethically right, particularly if telling Rachel the truth would cause her distress? Finding out what someone wants to happen is at the root of respect for autonomy and sometimes this is difficult for health care workers who may consider that the person in their care has not made the right decision. Holloway (2007) questions what she sees as a trend towards an uncritical application of the value of autonomy and argues that respecting the vulnerability of dying people as well as their autonomy contributes to ethical care practice.

In contemporary health care, with patients increasingly constructed as consumers and medicine constructed as a service industry subject to the disciplines of the market (Randall and Downie, 2000; 2006), patients are seen as having rights, specifically the right to have their autonomy respected. Robinson (2008, p. 30) develops this point more strongly, arguing that within health care 'autonomy of the patient or client is very much the cornerstone of any professional ethic'. What respecting autonomy might mean in cases where, for example, patients do not want to be told the full extent of their illness and likely outcome so that they can maintain hope (as in the case of Rachel) has implications for ethical professional practice (see also Jarrett and Payne, 2000). Although very much a study of its time, McIntosh (1977) found that many cancer patients would rather retain hope than know the truth. My own recent research (see Watts, 2009b) found similarly, with some cancer sufferers only willing to engage with palliative care discourses of life affirmation, taking care to avoid discussion of death. For example, Doris, a participant in my study, commenting on her resolve to regularly attend a cancer drop-in service offered by a hospice trust, told me 'it's not really like a hospice, it's more like a social club'. This reminded me that, for many, the term 'hospice' remains synonymous with death.

Woods (2007) has developed a useful framework with which to consider how autonomy might operate in practice, not just for patients with terminal diagnoses, but also for those with a range of health care needs. The framework comprises the four categorisations of best interests; wishes, preferences and choices; family concerns; and political/legal/social issues. All these have what Woods (2007, p. 110) refers to as 'boundary conditions' or limits, and these are considered below in order to draw out how these may impact on communication.

Woods (2007) suggests that the concept of *best interests* is multi-faceted, oscillating between objective and subjective taxonomies and closely allied to quality of life concerns. Twycross (2003, p.5) captures this simply but powerfully in the phrase 'quality of life is what a person says it is', suggesting that in respect of any medical intervention, what an individual may perceive to be in their best interests should be at the core of the decision-making process. Subjective best interests, however, have to be weighed against objective best interests that may include, for example, costs and effectiveness of treatments, and this forms part of the justice feature of Beauchamp and Childress's (2001) four principles model. The second categorisation of *wishes, preferences and choices* is closely linked to best interests and reflects the principle of autonomy that is both a capacity and moral principle. In the context of palliative care the *family*, as a third categorisation, adds to the complexity in the communication and decision-making process and, in some circumstances, can be seen to act as a condition to the autonomy of their ill relative. The case study of Rachel outlined above illustrates the point; it is Rachel's daughter rather than Rachel herself who has told the hospice staff that Rachel should not be told the truth about her situation.

Woods (2007), in this context, makes the point that sometimes, even within supportive and caring family networks, it can become necessary to defend the autonomy of the ill patient. The right of the family 'to know' or 'to be told' may not necessarily be in the best interests of the patient who can expect their confidentiality as well as their autonomy to be respected by health professionals. This returns us to a core feature of autonomy that is grounded in the free and uncoerced informed decision-making capacity of an individual. The fourth categorisation, *political/legal/social issues,* may act as a further condition on individual autonomy, and the outlawing of euthanasia is one example. The framework offered by Woods (2007) demonstrates how the concept of best interests informs the theory and practice of autonomy and is an integral component of decision-making and communication within health care. This framework, as a useful guide for practice, does not replace the need for each ethical encounter to be considered as an individual case in recognition that the 'blanket' application of general rules by health professionals is rarely likely to be an adequate response.

Some challenges for palliative care theory and practice

The above discussion illustrates the complex nature of contemporary palliative care both as a body of developing theory and as specialist professional practice. The extent to which the increasing specialisation and medicalisation of palliative care-giving is of benefit to patients and users of cancer services, and to the wider community as a whole, is the subject of current debate (Sinclair, 2007) and is of both theoretical and practical concern. Although space here does not allow for extensive discussion of this topic, the contribution made to this debate by Kellehear's (2005) development of a community model of health promoting palliative care, which challenges the primacy of the specialist clinical tradition in this area, merits attention.

The main principle that underpins this model is the idea that health care should be participatory, 'not something we *do to others* but a style of health care that we *do with others* (Randall and Downie, 2006, p. 25). This public health model is holistic and is rooted in an attempt to more strongly acknowledge the importance of social and cultural diversity, focusing as it does on the whole person as citizen, family member, carer, worker, and patient. Its emphasis is on both social care and community education to advance the thesis that we are all living with the prospect of death and that health promotion to enhance quality of life is relevant for individuals close to the end of life as well as throughout the life course. In particular, Kellehear (2005) argues for research and education to address wider community issues such as those related to the stigma and prejudice associated with dying (Howarth, 2007) and also as a way to counter a culture of death anxiety. This, he suggests, would serve to re-empower dying people and communities. These holistic values have great philosophical affinity with those of palliative care. However, community capacity building, as a central tenet of this model, may challenge the occupational capacity building that underpins the careers of palliative care professionals, giving rise to conceptual and practical tensions. Also, while death and loss are universal features of the human condition, this does not 'naturally' result in communitarian ownership of compassion and responsibility for the care of dying or bereaved people. Such care requires time and commitment, as part of a culture of acknowledged interdependence. Thus, although Kellehear's (2005) vision of community support for those who are dying requires further refinement and development in respect of its application, it does offer new ways of thinking about the delivery of all kinds of care within informal and non-professional networks.

One of the most pressing challenges for palliative care practice in the UK is widening its appeal and access to its services. Access to palliative care is not just a function of disease or geography (see Chapter Three for discussion of these factors); wider issues of social exclusion and disadvantage are significant and Koffman *et al.* (2008) consider these issues in terms of 'unmet need'. Although studies have found that a significant proportion of the UK population would prefer to die at home, this is much less likely to occur among the economically deprived, who are more likely to die younger and in a hospital setting (Koffman *et al.*, 2008). The case of offenders coping with life-limiting illness in prison (Bolger, 2004; Koffman *et al.*, 2008), where historically health care has been organised outside the NHS, presents particular challenges. The mutual distrust between prison staff and prisoners together with the difficulties of providing adequate symptom and pain relief in an environment where drugs to manage pain may also be appropriated for illicit purposes are some of the main factors. A further example of the complex web of disadvantage in relation to access to palliative care is the case of refugees and asylum seekers who may have problems accessing any health care (Blanche and Endersby, 2004). Koffman *et al.* (2008, p. 24) comment that the health problems for this group are exacerbated by 'family separation, hostility and racism from the host population, poverty and social isolation'.

A principal concern of practitioners and researchers in this area is that of the very low take-up of specialist palliative care services by black and minority ethnic (BME) communities (Smaje and Field, 1997). This stems in part from the Christian ethic as a driver for hospice development (see Chapter Three) that makes these institutions 'feel' inappropriate for many of other faiths. Koffman *et al.* (2008) make the general point that other barriers such as language and cultural differences may also prevent members of minority ethnic communities making use of specialist palliative care services. Firth (2004) provides a multi-dimensional explanatory framework for this phenomenon, citing ignorance about services, lack of information and contested understandings of the good death as central factors. For those of the Sikh or Hindu faith, for example, the prospect of a highly managed and controlled death that may involve the administration of opiates to reduce consciousness, is unacceptable and would severely compromise the meaning and quality of dying.

Palliative care, both as part of the hospice context and as provided in a range of community settings, continues to remain largely mono-cultural and, within an increasingly multi-cultural society, this clearly is an operational weakness. With this in mind, many hospices are attempting to address this issue and some have appointed multi-faith advisers. Gunaratnam (1997), however, cautions against the use of a simplistic fact-file approach to service development, arguing that culture is both dynamic and heterogeneous and that stereotypes can lure policy makers into making inappropriate decisions. The provision of culturally sensitive and appropriate palliative care to members of BME communities is taken up by Larkin (2008). He argues that there is a need for health practitioners to be 'contextually educated' but that this should be focused on the circumstances and needs of the individual. He makes the specific point that 'contextual education implies that textbook materials are only useful as resources for knowledge and not definitive guides to practice' (Larkin, 2008, p. 86). An example of contextual education is the study workshop entitled 'Palliative care for hard to reach groups' offered by a Scottish hospice and promoted by the Scottish Partnership for Palliative Care (SPPC website). This workshop and others listed are aimed not only at professional staff, but target health-care assistants and auxiliary staff in recognition of the importance of ongoing training and education for a wide range of health workers on culture and diversity issues.

As life expectancy increases we are seeing steadily growing numbers of very old and frail people, many with dementia, dying a slow death in different types of residential care settings. Many would benefit from palliative care interventions but, as Kellehear (2005) notes, there has been very little attention paid to the provision of this type of specialist care for this category of dying, mainly because historically care of the dying has been separated from the care of older people. Because much of palliative care practice focuses on clinical interventions for symptom control to enhance quality of life, with many of its resources devoted to relatively younger people (Koffman *et al.*, 2008, p. 20), large numbers of older people with dementia and associated physical deterioration who may be labelled as 'socially dead' (characterised by the loss of relationships) present a substantial challenge. Some might even argue that it is this 'group' of dying people who have been relegated to the ranks of the most disadvantaged in late modern society (McMurray, 2004). This further shortcoming of palliative care highlights how increasingly palliative care is seen as a clinically interventionist discipline with emphasis on social and spiritual care gradually receding. Within the discourse of professionalism caring for a person's spiritual needs is less tangible and thus more difficult to measure, particularly within a medical model that focuses on treatment (Cobb, 2001).

For professional carers the terminal phase of disease, particularly in the case of cancer, is a time of certainty (Walter, 1994, p. 144). It is also a time when users of palliative care services (who may have been dying for a long time) make the transition from home care to institutionalised care (Lawton, 2000; Armstrong-Coster, 2004) with death medically managed in ways differently from home deaths (Ball *et al.*, 1996). Central to this transition is the locus of control with patients at this stage of deterioration often very weak, and lapsing in and out of consciousness. The extent to which patients can retain control of their care and have their needs met at this very end stage, which in some cases includes requests to their carers to hasten their death, is a function of the particular setting, the family's involvement and the responses of individual carers (Lawton, 2000). Within hospices this response may include the palliative sedation of the dying and almost certainly will necessitate high levels of personal nursing care. This 'end comfort' work, when uncertainty is over, can be very satisfying to nursing staff and valued by the dying and their families (Walter, 1994). Specialist palliative care settings, with good patient/staff ratios can offer this, whereas general hospitals are less able to cater for this level of intensive and individualised nursing care as death approaches. There are relatively few in-patient beds available in hospices and this has brought increasing pressure to develop specialist palliative care skills in other care settings. The provision of appropriate training, however, is a resource issue within a cash-starved NHS.

Concerns about equity and access to palliative care have been discussed above citing the piecemeal development of hospices as an important factor; this is discussed in more detail in the next chapter. The concepts of effectiveness and efficiency also have a strategic element and are tied to a market model that has its 'home' within the culture of business/economic management. Palliative care cannot escape its reach, particularly in relation to institutional provision that increasingly has come under the control of the NHS. Care of the dying, however, does not easily lend itself to quantitative measurement because of its creative and responsive nature as part of a patient-led service with quality as a central focus. In this sense palliative care may become the victim of its own (albeit narrow) success with lack of transparency of resource/outcomes ratios perceived as an operational weakness.

CHAPTER 3

Hospice Development in the UK

The discussion of palliative care philosophy and practice in the previous chapter pointed to their wide application within hospitals, care homes and in individuals' own homes in the community. Despite the increasing use of palliative care in these health and community settings, the inextricable link in the public mind between palliative care and hospices remains strong, mainly because hospices are seen as the institutional and symbolic home of palliative care. The term *hospice* usually refers to a residential facility to which terminally ill patients are admitted for both symptom management and care during the end stage of their illness. However, most hospice care (usually undertaken by teams of specialist palliative care nurses who are based at a hospice) increasingly now takes place in the community in patients' homes with family members and district nurses as principal caregivers. Hospices act as a community-based institutional 'hub' for a range of specialist expertise and services. They co-ordinate education and training for professionals involved in delivering end-of-life care and are committed to an interdisciplinary approach, which is a central principle of palliative care philosophy. Thus hospices employ social workers, art therapists and chaplains alongside specialist nurses and doctors.

Much has been written about the development of the modern hospice movement, particularly the pioneering efforts of its founder, Cicely Saunders, who formulated the vision of a haven where people could experience relief from pain and die with dignity within an atmosphere of calm and tranquillity. The services offered under the 'umbrella' of hospice are outlined below to draw out the diverse components of the end-of-life care they offer, characterised by

Saunders as a 'high person, low technology and hardware system of health care' (DeSpelder and Strickland, 2005).

A brief history of the hospice movement

The contemporary hospice movement has inherited a mixed history with the early concept of hospice in Europe finding representation in the form of shelters for travellers and pilgrims as well as the itinerant poor in the twelfth and thirteenth centuries (Clark and Seymour, 1999). The hospice at Jerusalem, for example, at around 1165 had 2000 beds and was rooted in social approaches to the care of the sick and the dying (Kellehear, 2005). This kind of collective care of the dying was part of a community model that predates the history of professional care of the dying (Kellehear, 2005, p. 2), with whole community involvement a significant feature. Kellehear (2005, p. 13) reinforces this point, arguing that 'care of the dying was a normal and routine matter for families and communities'.

It was not until the mid-nineteenth century that we see the development of more specialist settings for care of the dying alongside the rise of modern medicine. Kellehear (2005) explains that formal care of the dying developed gradually from a longer history of community care, based not in cities or large towns, but in villages and hamlets where a majority of the population lived. Examples of the emerging formalisation are the opening of Harold's Cross Hospice in Dublin in 1879 and St Joseph's Hospice in Hackney in 1905. The establishment of these hospices can be seen as important markers in the formalisation of institutionalised end-of-life care in industrial society. As the names of these early modern hospices illustrate, this new therapeutic institution carried both religious and philanthropic overtones and operated on the basis of the principle of segregation (Sinclair, 2007), specifically the segregation of the dying from their normal community so that they could be offered special-ised dedicated care. However, although retaining their religious foundation, these early modern hospices did signal the start of a shift in the context of death and dying from the religious to the medical, though not promoting a prescribed or particular way of dying. Rather they sought to create an environ-ment in which the process of dying could be lived in a manner that accorded with the needs and beliefs of the dying person.

It was the pioneering work of Cicely Saunders, however, in establishing St Christopher's in 1967 in South London as the first modern research and teaching hospice to cater specifically for the needs of the dying, who raised the profile of terminal care. Previously end-of-life care had been peripheral to the agenda of the medical profession, mainly due to associated discourses of death as failure. The development of the modern hospice movement has primarily been born out of a Christian tradition imbued with the principle of duty that can also be understood as a form of social control of the poor (Clark and Seymour, 1999, p. 69). This sense of duty goes some way towards explaining the importance of the volunteer workforce to different aspects of hospice activities (Andersson and Ohlen, 2005). Sinclair (2007, p. 49), commenting on the pronounced voluntary staff component of most hospices, suggests that the population at large sees palliative care and the possibility of hospice support as a gift, and one to be both earned or repaid. This notwithstanding, volunteer work in this setting can be both stressful and emotionally demanding and can lead to 'burn-out' as may occur among members of the professional hospice workforce (Dein and Abbas, 2005).

In-patient hospices are the original model of palliative care delivery and by the year 2000 Britain had 400 hospices and palliative care units helping to provide a new model of death (Jupp and Walter, 1999). By the year 2008 this number had risen to 716, with only 15 dedicated hospices located in Scotland (Help the Hospices, personal communication, 23 October 2008). Clark (1993) comments that, although hospice is often described as a philosophy rather than a place (particularly by US commentators), the drive to build more hospices and establish professionally led dedicated palliative care units is very striking. Sinclair (2007) argues that this is hardly surprising given the primacy of the institutional model in establishing status, authority and credibility within the medical mainstream. Added to this, the design of hospices as dedicated care spaces where death is 'diagnosed, announced and attended', has led to architects thinking afresh about the hospice as a new building type in the light of the right to a 'good death' becoming a new social demand (Worpole, 2009).

The expansion in the number of hospices, although ad hoc (Field and Addington-Hall, 2000) and therefore unevenly geographically distributed, has been significant and widespread. Hospices are now well established as the principal site for the practice of specialist palliative care and have traditionally operated outside direct mainstream NHS control with many constituted as charities dependent largely on fundraising initiatives for their income. Although mainly charity-based, hospices now operate on a business model raising funds from corporate sponsors as well as from second-hand shops and community donations using collection boxes. Despite the continuing drive to maintain some autonomy, the independent feature of their operation is gradually being eroded within a culture of audit and evidence-based practice, as hospices are increasingly expected to demonstrate the effectiveness of services as part of the NHS referral system (Randall and Downie, 2006).

Given the fear of cancer in the public mind, many hospices have been able to rely on a fairly constant stream of emotional giving (including legacies) together with other types of corporate donations. With dedicated cancer giving most hospices have continued to focus heavily on cancer care, although some now admit patients with AIDS, multiple sclerosis, end-stage renal failure and motor neurone disease (Addington-Hall, 2004). It is difficult to gain accurate figures for non-cancer hospice admissions but a study by Kite *et al.* (1999) that considered 421 hospice admissions found that only 4% of these were for patients with a non-cancer diagnosis. This targeted giving has been influential in framing hospice care as a form of privileged care for some dying people while others are almost completely excluded from access to this support. The issue of equity has been discussed in Chapter Two as part of the debate about extending palliative care to all. However it is important to re-visit this here in respect of funding for hospice care, which continues to be heavily focused on cancer sufferers, who make up 95% of patient referrals for specialist palliative care (Payne and Seymour, 2004). With the increase in state funding of hospices we may see a reduction in this burden of prescription in terms of disease focus.

The original ideal of hospice, as the setting for a good death, is the creation of an extended family (Howarth, 2007) to act as a refuge or safe retreat for the dying and those close to them. Patients are encouraged to pursue their interests and pleasures as they would in their own home and, with extensive visiting hours, to spend as much time as they wish with friends and family members. Extending this familial idea, hospices see the patient's family as an integral part of the unit of care, involving them in all aspects of decision-making. The importance of the family is a recurring theme in the literature on the culture of hospice care, offering insight into the ways in which these institutions approach support of the dying as one aspect of the holistic approach they advocate. This familial feature is especially pronounced in hospices dedicated to the care of children and young people and in recent years a number of these have been established across the UK to respond to what has been perceived as the special needs of families looking after a child with a life-limiting condition. The organisation Children's Hospices UK reports that there are now 41 children's hospices in the UK, of which two are located in Scotland.

In summary, the modern hospice has developed as a critique of acute hospitals where the emphasis is on medical and technological innovation and intervention in pursuit of cure and the prolongation of life (Howarth, 2007). In contrast, the hospice model of care is grounded in the principles of palliative care, which accept death as a normal part of life (Koffman *et al.*, 2008). Clark and Seymour (1999, p. 107) make the point that staff working in hospice environments are sometimes characterised as doing so as a response to a particular 'vocational calling'. This work has now grown into a global social movement with different levels of hospice provision now available in many countries in Australasia, the Americas and the Indian sub-continent, with African countries showing the lowest level of uptake (Wright *et al.*, 2006). Space here does not allow for an extensive discussion of the possible reasons for the variable uptake of hospice services in some parts of the world but this may, in part, be explained by cultural issues that render the Western model of institutional hospice care inappropriate. For example, within some societies end-of-life care is seen as the responsibility of the family rather than an institution and cultural differences in attitudes between service providers and the communities they serve can be the source of suspicion and mistrust.

The contrast of hospice with mainstream medical approaches to death and dying has been challenged by some commentators (notably James and Field, 1992; Kellehear, 2005) who highlight ways in which specialist palliative care within hospices has evolved into a clinical set of disciplines whose emphasis on pain control and symptom management is similar to that found in mainstream clinical settings. Kellehear (2005) makes the specific point that increasingly the focus of hospice work has moved from accompanying the dying to an orientation where treatment interventions and the development of services are the key goals. At the core of Kellehear's (2005, p. 21) thesis is what he sees as the 'professionalisation of relations' with caregivers positioned as experts and patients as clients, the 'receivers' of that expert knowledge. James and Field (1992) support this point with their claim that in parallel with the rise in the number of hospices there has been a 'reprofessionalisation' of end-of-life care. Bradshaw (1996) and Watts (2008) both make a similar point in relation to professional spiritual care-giving which, they argue, has become little more than an empty standardised exercise in the application of skills and techniques. This point will be developed further in the next chapter, which considers how spirituality is understood within the domain of professional health care and how this shapes both policy and practice in relation to spiritual care-giving.

Hospice care in Scotland

Health care in Scotland is delivered under the aegis of fourteen NHS Boards which have overall responsibility for end–of-life care services. Just as in other parts of the UK, in Scotland the voluntary and charity sectors have played a significant role in supporting and funding the development of hospices and there are now 15 of these located across Scotland, some serving highly dispersed local populations. The charity The Children's Hospice Association Scotland (CHAS) was established to provide hospice services in Scotland for children and young people with life-limiting conditions. In Scotland there are an estimated 1,200 children with a life-limiting/life-threatening condition and over half will require active palliative care (CHAS, 2005). Under the aegis of CHAS, Rachel House Hospice in Kinross opened in March 1996 as the first Scottish children's hospice. Robin House in Balloch, opened in August 2005, is the second and together they can provide ongoing support for up to three hundred families and seventeen hospice nights per year for each family. These two hospices have purpose-built family facilities and Rachel House, for example, can accommodate at any one time up to eight children and their families who need palliative care. Families can refer themselves for support and this may be at the point of disease diagnosis, at mid-point in the disease process or at the end stages of life. In addition to in-patient care, both hospices operate a CHAS at Home Team care service to families across Scotland providing care in their own homes when needed.

In 2006/7 the majority of specialist palliative care beds (250 beds) and 72% of day care places were provided by voluntary hospices, as reported in a review of palliative care services in Scotland carried out by the Scottish Partnership for Palliative Care and submitted to the Auditor General for Scotland in August 2008 (SPPC, 2007). This review expressed concern about the lack of a co-ordinated approach to end-of-life care in Scotland; of particular concern was the significant variation across Scotland in the availability of specialist palliative care services and the difficulties patients with complex needs may have in accessing these. This concern has given rise to a number of policy initiatives that are outlined in Chapter Seven.

Patients with cancer currently account for 90% of specialist palliative care activity in Scotland although cancer accounts for less than 30% of all deaths (SPPC, 2007); patients with other conditions such as motor neurone disease, multiple sclerosis and organ failure do not have equal access to the same services. The emphasis on cancer is partly because the awareness of palliative care needs and the development of specialist palliative care expertise have historically been linked with the needs of cancer patients. The requirement to address the continuing focus on cancer-related services (as is the case in the rest of the UK) is now considered a priority so that people living with and dying from a range of other conditions can benefit from a palliative approach to their care. Issues of access are not only determined by disease category, and the SPPC 2007 review found that hospices and NHS boards are not able to demonstrate that different ethnic and social groups have equal access to specialist palliative care services since they do not routinely monitor who uses these services.

The review noted that of the £59 million spent on specialist palliative care almost half came from the voluntary sector mainly in relation to the funding of the 15 independent hospices. Another finding documented in the review was that most palliative care in Scotland is provided by generalist staff in hospitals, care homes or in patients' own homes (as is the case across the UK) and that these generalist practitioners need increased skills training from specialists in order to improve the quality of care for patients. Generalists reported that they felt better equipped to support the physical needs of their palliative care patients than their psychosocial or spiritual needs. Of further note is that the level of specialist palliative care activity provided in hospitals is not recorded by the NHS boards, and that the costs of generalist palliative care cannot easily be separated out from mainstream services. The key findings of this review suggest that we currently have an unclear picture of the scope, costs and effectiveness of palliative care provision in Scotland across a range of settings, including hospices. This lack of clarity, together with the associated need for defined policy objectives, provides the focus of Chapter Seven.

Hospice day care

Day care, as one type of provision within most hospice services, has its own practice territory with wide variations now well documented in the literature. The support offered within day care focuses on enhancing the quality of life of patients through the provision of information, rehabilitation, physiotherapy and occupational therapy with the management and monitoring of symptoms central to psychosocial support (Myers and Hearn, 2001; Dosser and Nicol, 2006). Coping with what O'Connor (2004, p. 126) describes as 'transitions in status from wellness to illness, illness to wellness' is very much a feature of palliative day care, which Clark and Seymour (1999) note can sometimes act as a 'stepping stone' to hospice in-patient admission. Lawton (2000) identifies a further aim of day care as the provision of a safe environment in which patients can accept and share the impact of life-threatening illness. Borrowing from Maslow (1970), the need to belong is a basic characteristic of what it means to be human, and this can often be met through talking with others in a similar situation who have shared concerns. This can lead to the development of an informal network for the exchange of information in ways similar to in-patient settings (see, for example, McIntosh, 1977).

Day care, however, is not unique to palliative care and builds on practice now well established in the care of older people, those with learning disabilities and more widely as part of psychiatric services (Myers and Hearn, 2001). Within palliative day care a high priority is placed on meeting individual needs, enhancing quality of life by promoting independence, providing psycho-social support to manage anxiety and depression, relief of social isolation and the engendering of hope (Higginson *et al.*, 2000; Kennett, 2000; Myers and Hearn, 2001). From a review of 40 palliative day care centres, Higginson *et al.* (2000) found that the most common activities in pursuit of the above objectives were review of patients' symptoms or needs, bathing, wound care, physiotherapy, hairdressing and aromatherapy. Additionally, in some of the centres, patients were able to participate in art and music therapy, trips/days out and a range of creative and leisure activities led by a mix of professionals and volunteers.

In their study of hospice day care, Higginson *et al.* (2000) identified two principal types of day centres: those that described themselves as more medically oriented (with greater attention paid to patients' physical needs) and those that described themselves as more socially oriented (with stronger emphasis on patients' informational and social needs). In both categories most patients attended for less than a year and 30 of the centres operated a discharge policy that other research suggests could have negative impacts on patients having to break attachments to this social group (Richardson *et al.*, 2001). A majority had one or more clinicians running the day centre and all used the services of volunteers to support the activities offered. Though not exhaustive, this study offers a useful profile of how palliative day care in the UK is constituted and organised, painting a picture of a diverse and complex model of care that Wilkes *et al.* (1978) argue can act as a rallying point for patients and families. Across these two models, friendship, creative and therapeutic activities (see von Hornstein and Gruber, 2006) and social interaction contribute to a flexible resource that is increasingly being scrutinised in terms of cost (Douglas *et al.*, 2003), audit and evaluation (Higginson, 1998).

Commenting on the issue of evaluation, Higginson and Goodwin (2001, p. 12) correctly assert that the 'effectiveness of a service is the extent to which it matches the demands and needs of the population'. Assessing patients' needs within day care is essential in planning and delivering services and in determining the effectiveness of what is provided. This, however, has been shown to be a particularly difficult area, not least because attendance can fluctuate as a function of the unpredictable health of patients and communication with other services may not be comprehensive (O'Keefe, 2001).

As discussed in the previous chapter, the whole area of audit and effectiveness within palliative care has come under scrutiny (Hearn, 2001) with Barker and Hawkett (2004, p. 717) arguing that 'all health care delivery must have clear standards which are evidence-based, and encompass the concepts of equity, access, effectiveness and efficiency'. Despite palliative care's reputation for high quality individualised care this framework points to a systematic objective rather than subjective audit of palliative care to prove its effectiveness in line with other health and social care services. However, the successes of palliative care are captured mainly in the narratives of individuals and are anecdotal, and this is especially the case within the hospice day care setting where the benefits of social intercourse and creative and complementary therapies are difficult to measure. With regard to complementary therapies, their value, in terms of measurable benefit to patients, has been the focus of a number of studies (see, for example, Wilcock *et al.*, 2004) that suggest that the evidence base for their continued provision within day care is contested. In respect of organisational aspects, the literature also draws attention to other issues such as the role of the doctor within day care (Tookman and Scharpen-von Heussen, 2001; White and Johnson, 2004), the use of an appointments-based day care system (Low *et al.*, 2005) and the mischaracterisation of day care (Dosser and Nicol, 2006). The continuing debate in the literature about the form and value of day care (see Myers, 2001) illustrates the increasing importance within a rationalised health care system of the need to demonstrate efficiency and 'value for money', much of which is measured by the achievement of targets.

In summary, some of these threads are drawn together by Jeffrey (2005), who argues that quality care of the dying is comprised of many invisible components and that this type of care may be under threat because of the current performance and target culture, with day care particularly vulnerable due to its perceived position as an optional extra.

The future of the hospice movement

As hospices have become more regulated and subject to the processes of audit and evaluation, they have become forced to deal with the challenge of excessive bureaucracy, which can lead to a routinisation of care (DeSpelder and Strickland, 2005). Howarth (2007, p. 143) identifies increased hierarchy within hospice organisation as one consequence of bureaucratisation, noting that, in the early modern hospice, nurses were able to diagnose and prescribe medication but that now there has been a return to traditional patterns of job demarcation with evidence of a growing culture of managerialism. Some might argue that this is due, at least in part, to the rise of a litigious society, which is at the root of much defensive practice across many professions.

In the early pioneering phase of modern day hospice development, the vocational work of end-of-life care was characterised by a strong ideological imperative based on hospice as a radical and much improved alternative to hospitals with 'better dying' as a key goal and a 'good death' as the ultimate value. However, as has been discussed above, if hospices become just another medical option for terminal care, the movement may find it difficult to practically sustain its philosophical commitment to total care of the dying person and their family, with holistic values giving way to pragmatic medical priorities. Clark (1999) develops this critique, arguing that one consequence of total care may be total control with the medical management of death the goal of hospice professionals.

The focus on the growing medicalisation of hospice is taken up by Lawton (2000), who has challenged the reality of a hospice 'good death'. In her ethnography of a UK hospice she found that it was only patients with extreme and unmanageable physical symptoms who were admitted as in-patients to the hospice, which, she says, was the setting for extreme agitation, vomiting, incontinence and loss of autonomy among its dying patients. All these aspects contribute to a form of 'dirty dying' associated with 'unbounded' bodies that, Lawton (2000) argues, is rarely spoken about. Armstrong-Coster (2004) supports some of Lawton's observations, highlighting the tensions between the 'difficult' and 'raging' bodies of those in the final stages of their illness and hospice staff wanting to present an appropriately serene and controlled stage for dying. In Armstrong-Coster's (2004) study the issue of acceptance of their dying by hospice in-patients appeared to contribute variously to positive/negative outcomes. She notes that some people dying of cancer choose hospital rather than hospice care in the terminal phase specifically because hope and cure are associated with hospitals while death is seen as the expected outcome of hospice admission. Theirs is a very different picture to that painted by the wider hospice fraternity, described by Lofland (1978) as part of the 'happy death movement'.

With many hospices now concentrating their efforts in the community, as part of a broader health initiative to enable old and very ill people to remain in their own homes for as long as possible, there has been a reduction in the number of hospice in-patient beds available. This suggests that institutional provision may only be able to respond to very end stage illness and only that with a defined short-term prognosis. Furthermore, the management of dying, as part of the trend towards medicalisation, is likely to be more high-tech with ever more sophisticated drug interventions, making this an elite form of dying available only to the very few and in the main only to those dying of cancer.

These issues are taken up by Lamers (2002), who argues that three different types of hospice may begin to emerge, each providing different levels of care. The first would offer traditional hospice care for people with definable short-term prognoses, as would be the case with incurable cancers. A second type of provision would be long-term care for people with an indeterminate diagnosis who do not require expensive drug interventions to manage symptoms to improve quality of life as, for example, in the case of those suffering from Alzheimer's disease. The third category is the high-tech hospice for people who require expensive sophisticated therapies to maintain reasonable relief of symptoms in the face of an uncertain prognosis, as may apply with advanced AIDS. To date this tripartite model of hospice sub-specialisation has not begun to be piloted either in the UK or in other countries, but some measure of organisational change may be required if hospices are to meet the challenges of providing high quality end-of-life care in the face of diverse needs.

As with palliative care discussed in the previous chapter, the utilisation of hospice services by members of minority ethnic communities across the UK is very low, even in areas where they comprise the majority population – and this despite major recent efforts to widen access to include these groups. This therefore raises the question of whether the vision of individualised responsiveness espoused by the hospice movement is being realised, particularly in relation to those whose values may be experienced as challenging. Groups who favour patriarchal decision-making or where informed consent for women falls outside cultural norms are two examples. Access to the full range of relevant end-of-life services (pain control and symptom management, respite care and bereavement support) by all users is an issue of social justice but providing these in culturally appropriate ways and settings continues to challenge the wider hospice movement. Smaje and Field (1997) argue that the model of service delivery that is likely to meet with most success is a collaborative one where palliative care professionals work closely and sensitively with service users and local community/faith groups to integrate services within existing community structures. They argue that 'this requires an appreciation not only of different cultural beliefs and ways of living but also of the ways in which the wider social structures of British society affect and shape the lifestyles and life chances of minority ethnic group members' (Smaje and Field, 1997, p. 162). Gunaratnam (2008), however, warns against the prescription of models of cultural competence as a response to the end-of-life care needs of minority ethnic service users, as these may be given primacy over personalised care with the potential for emotional pain resulting from social exclusion.

As a closing reflection on this topic, Richard Smith (2000), commenting in the *British Medical Journal*, highlights the paradoxical nature of specialist palliative care, as provided by hospices, for a universal eventuality. He points to the trend for the lessons learned in hospice and palliative care about the importance of managing the total pain of a dying person to be reclaimed by everyone, in all areas of health care practice. This position has resonance with the health-promoting palliative care approach advocated by Kellehear (2005), which argues for a community rather than a specialist professional model of care of dying people as outlined in the previous chapter. While hospices may continue to drive and develop specialist palliative care practice through extensive education and training programmes (almost as providers of expert consultancy to the end-of-life care workforce), the trend towards generalists learning and applying specialist knowledge and skills in general and community health and social care settings looks set to continue. Increasingly we are seeing hospice care associated with patients who have complex symptoms that require expert management and with very end stage care where life is measured in days rather than weeks or months. Recognition of the importance of individual spirituality at this time has been widely documented and Chapter Four has this as its central theme.

CHAPTER 4

Spirituality

As discussed in Chapters Two and Three, palliative care philosophy acknowl-edges the importance of spiritual values and beliefs in contributing to making us who we are. Beliefs provide a dependable framework of meaning within which people are able to make sense of their lives (Cobb, 2008) and the func-tion of religious and spiritual coping in adjustment to serious illness has been increasingly recognised. In particular, there has been growing interest in the importance of understanding and valuing patients' individual spirituality as a function of providing appropriate support, particularly as part of nursing practice. New ways to both assess and address spiritual concerns as part of overall quality of life are being developed by health care practitioners as part of a package of support for people with critical and terminal illness (Randall and Downie, 2006; Watts, 2008). For this support to be meaningful, however, it is necessary to determine which dimensions of spirituality are relevant and the ways in which the human spirit can be celebrated in the face of life-threatening illness (Cobb and Legood, 2008). The ultimate value of such exploration is to make it possible for us to die the way we live (Hockey, 2002).

Spirituality is a contested concept with a wide taxonomy of meaning discussed in the literature. This chapter will explore understandings of the concept with particular focus on the connections between spirituality and health and the importance of spirituality to personal well-being. The perceived 'duty' on the part of health professionals, particularly nurses, to support the spiritual needs of patients has been challenged by some writers and this debate will provide the focus of the last part of the chapter.

Defining spirituality

The discussion that follows will consider spirituality from a number of perspectives, including spirituality as religious belief and practice, as existen-tial meaning, as a quest for universal inter-connectedness (Thorne, 2005) and as self-worth based on Giddens's (1991, p. 57) concept of ontological security. This concept can be understood as a sense an individual has about continuity in their life that brings assurance and trust in the future. The relationship between spirituality and health, particularly in the context of life-threatening illness, will be a focus of the second discussion topic drawing principally on ideas presented in the nursing literature, which explores the topic mainly as a vehicle for developing professional health care practice.

The term 'spirituality' is characterised by its conceptual complexity and plurality. The conceptual range includes its distinction from religion (Rumbold, 2002) and its place at the core of individual lived experience as an underpinning feature of personhood (Moore and Purton, 2006), so that spirituality may be expressed both in a religious and a humanistic context (Wright, 2004). The concept of spirituality is present in all cultures and is generally understood to encompass experiential aspects, whether related to religious adherence and membership of a religious group or to acknowledging a wider sense of peace and connectedness. Individuals may thus consider themselves as spiritual and religious, highly valuing religious faith as the lens through which they understand the meaning of life. Others may regard themselves as spiritual but not religious, highly valuing spiritual well-being but not as part of a religious path, with this latter category reflecting the shift from sacralisation to secularisation within a postmodern post-industrial context. Whether as part of religious or secular traditions, the spiritual domain acknowledges the importance of the big questions of life and death, in relation to self, others and the 'cosmos' (Wright, 2004).

Across time and cultures spirituality has been allied to religion, particularly formal institutionalised religion with its emphasis on theist and doctrinal principles that can be understood as orthodoxy (Cobb, 2001). Religion is highly culturally and socially determined. Robinson (2008, p. 50) defines religion as 'a system of faith and practice expressing a particular spirituality'; this system, he argues, is predicated on the features of community and corporate awareness of the ultimate *other* or God. Within a religious framework, although spirituality will find individual interpretation, its meaning is revealed and renewed through the narrative of the community. Because of its group structures, religion tends to be prescriptive, maintaining collective congruence and a sense of spiritual belonging that transcends everyday material or sensory experience. Acts of meditation or worship are spiritual practices that 'bind' members of faith communities where the position of 'self' is less important than the cohesion of the group.

In recent times, with the widespread decline in adherence to formal religion, particularly in many countries in the West, alternative, mainly secular meanings of spirituality have found prominence in the literature. Rumbold (2002, p. 9) points to the increasing authority of the self, rather than the collective, as one explanation for the renewed interest in non-religious spirituality. He makes the further claim that spirituality has become instrumental in enabling individuals to assert their own personal authority to carve for themselves a pathway of life meaning that can both embrace and reject authoritarian values. The authority of a specific, often religious, tradition now increasingly gives way to the authority of the individual *over* those traditions. The intersection of micro and macro values makes possible new forms of creativity in the search for understanding who we are and why we are here. Cobb (2001) character-ises these concerns about the essential questions of life meaning as 'ultimate values', claiming that these are at the core of spirituality because it is these values that are fundamental in framing the world of the individual.

This 'fundamental' attribute receives much comment in the wider spirituality literature, as does the claim to universality with, for example, McSherry (2000, p. 27) arguing that spirituality is a 'universal concept relevant to all individu-als'. Zohar and Marshall (2001, p. 4) argue that human beings are defined by a universal longing to find meaning and value in what they do and experience, while Clarkson (2002, p. 2) develops this to claim that 'human beings will die (and do die) from loss of meaning more violently than from hunger, illness or deprivation'. Clarkson's (2002) reference to loss of meaning involves a sense of 'alienated dying', with individuals increasingly alienated from one another and the world. Dissatisfied with materialism and feeling disconnected from a greater whole they experience a sense of inner loneliness. With the developing emphasis in the West on secular and individually based forms of spirituality, the loss of community (a core feature of religion as discussed above) may be a significant component of the loneliness and spiritual isolation identified by Clarkson (2002). It is this potential for spiritual alienation that has been taken up within palliative care practice, with health professionals enjoined to address spiritual concerns with their patients.

A life-threatening illness can raise the prospect of being disconnected from the embodied self previously recognised as 'me' (Holstein and Gubrium, 2000). Giddens's (1991) concept of ontological security, which describes this fear, is relevant here and contributes to existential understandings of spiritu-ality. Ontological security derives from a sense of continuity with regard to an individual's life events. It is framed by a sense of order within which people are able to give meaning to their lives. To be ontologically secure is to understand one's place in the world and is a prerequisite for the sense of self-worth and self-identity that Giddens argues is not simply given, but must be routinely created, renewed and sustained in the activities of the individual. This understanding of 'self' is therefore a narrative that establishes the continuity of an individual's existence as him or herself. In the context of those facing life-threatening illness, these core values that constitute ontological security can be undermined to produce what Bury (1982) terms a 'biographical disruption'. This can result in individuals questioning their role and purpose in life as they both see themselves and are seen by others as changed by the experience of illness.

Spirituality and health

In recent years some writers have directed their attention to the ways in which the search for universal meaning can be conceptualised as applied spirituality, particularly within education and health care (Robinson, 2008). A number of scholars working in these areas ascribe the search for universal meaning to an innate physiological-biological foundation (Buttery and Robertson, 2005; McSherry, 2006) with some making claims for the benefits of incorporating spirituality within mental health programmes to enhance well-being (Pargament et al., 2005; Swinton, 2001). For older people, a sense of identity and understanding of a person's place and status in the world appear to constitute key components of spirituality (Thompson, 2007). This may have practice and policy implications in respect of effective long-term care and social support provided to increasing numbers of the very elderly in many countries in the West.

The nursing canon has been particularly influential in this area and has made a major contribution to understandings of spirituality in the context of health. For example, McSherry and Cash (2004), writing in the nursing tradition, present a taxonomy of meaning of spirituality across a continuum with religious and theist ideals at one extreme, and secular, humanistic and existential elements at the other. They conclude that nursing is constructing an overarching 'blanket' definition of spirituality to accommodate what they see as the increasingly diverse human and spiritual needs of those in their care. Writing earlier on this theme, Walter (1997; 2002) focuses on health care's developing interest in the spiritual, drawing attention to the human and the emotional as a contrast to institutionalised systems that are driven by financial rationality and medicalisation. The heightened emphasis on the individual and the subjective within Walter's critique points to a broadly liberal and interpretive spirituality that is culturally inscribed but not theistically bound, with this model responsive to the trend towards secularisation and its application in a range of care settings (Heelas *et al.*, 2005). For those developing policy in this area, the importance of acknowledging a wide spiritual plurality that takes account of secular as well as faith beliefs is increasingly emphasised.

The literature suggests that at the end of life meanings of spirituality come into sharper focus, both for the dying person and their caregivers. Kellehear (2000) has developed a tripartite multidimensional model of spiritual needs for those in the dying phase and this has been useful in helping to clarify categories of spiritual needs and domains of experience. He identifies situational needs (purpose, hope, affirmation, mutuality, connectedness and social presence); moral and biographical needs (peace and reconciliation, reunion, prayer, forgiveness and closure); and religious needs (religious reconciliation, divine forgiveness, religious rites, clerical support, religious literature and discussion). These dimensions have instrumental value in developing understanding of different forms of spirituality together with the possible ways of addressing different spiritual needs. Another facet to the spiritual dimension of human experience is 'inter-connectedness'. Thorne (2005, p. 6) explains that '[the term] spiritual is commonly used by those who wish to affirm their belief in an overarching reality which points to the inter-connectedness of the created order and to a perception of the human being as essentially mysterious and not ultimately definable in biological, psychological or sociological terms'.

Drawing these threads together from the literature, we find that spirituality emerges largely as a concept devoid of religion, an instrument to enhance personal well-being, and a tool with which to improve or maintain health and quality of life (Sinclair *et al.*, 2006). The search for new forms of spiritual meaning in Western societies is based on a rejection of both the materialism of science and of the commodification of society (Howarth, 2007, p. 100). This search also derives from widespread disenchantment with the collectivist and prescriptive structures of established religions. The increasingly positive evaluation of spirituality above formal adherence to religion appears to be linked to the valuing of personal experience, relationships and secular as well as faith belief systems that afford empowerment and transcendence. The fluidity of the spiritual domain with a resulting 'deregulated' spirituality, which can include dimensions of self, others, higher beings and the cosmos as well as the activities of being, finding meaning, connecting and transcending, points to its inherent plurality and subjectivity. At risk of the charge of reductionism, it may be useful to close this critique of the differing spirituality frameworks by referring readers to the thinking of Mitchell *et al.* (2008, p. 101), who offer a simple overarching definition of spirituality that they characterise as 'the means by which humans satisfy the need to transcend or rise above the everyday material or sensory experience'.

What is spiritual care?

Given that the spiritual is no longer the sole prerogative of religion, the responsibility for the spiritual well-being of individuals, particularly at times of illness, crisis and loss, is increasingly seen as a shared concern with professions such as nursing, social work, counselling and psychotherapy. With the assumption that spirituality is a fundamental dimension of the human person and of human experience, these professions are now emphasising spirituality as an essential element in their practice, with the nursing profession leading discussion of 'best practice' in this area (Dyson *et al.*, 1997; McSherry, 2006; Tanyi, 2002). The application of theory to practice, however, appears to be fragmented, not least because meanings of spirituality and how these might inform the delivery of spiritual care remain a contested area (Peberdy, 2000). This notwithstanding, all components of care have increasingly become associated with the discourse of 'patient-centredness', aimed at respecting autonomy and individual choice (Wright, 2004), acknowledging that 'one size does not fit all'. In pursuit of high quality personalised spiritual care, Stoll (1979) documents the way in which nurses have in the past been advised to construct a spiritual history of their patients by questioning them about their understanding of 'god', hope and the significance to them of faith practices. The idea that spiritual values can be neatly and conveniently identified, categorised and responded to in ways similar to those of disease diagnosis and treatment is now acknowledged as problematic, although vestiges of this can still be traced within the 'audit culture' that now dominates UK health care delivery (Peberdy, 2000).

The model of patient-centred care, as discussed in the previous two chapters, has been incorporated within the professional discourse of specialist palliative care practice that has its roots in the hospice movement (Wright, 2004; Randall and Downie, 2006). Palliative care philosophy places the spiritual dimension of care as central to the holding together of physical, social and psychological aspects of well-being and argues for interventionist spiritual care plans to operate in parallel with other care plans to reduce suffering. Inclusive models of spiritual care that resonate with concepts of holism and the values of acceptance and non-judgemental compassion are widely discussed within palliative care literature (see, for example, Clark and Seymour, 1999; Wright, 2004), recognising that patients are drawn from pluralistic cultural backgrounds. The actual 'doing' of spiritual care, either by health professionals or by informal caregivers, is the subject of widespread comment in the literature and discussion of a range of approaches now follows.

Drawing on the broad understanding of spirituality outlined above as the 'valuing of the non-material aspects of life' (Mitchell *et al.*, 2008), Twycross (2003, p. 38) offers insight into what spiritual care at the end of life might mean, outlining a range of appropriate interventions and behaviours. He suggests that affirmation and acceptance of the person in a non-judgemental way together with achieving forgiveness and reconciliation, as a form of completion, are core components of spiritual care of the dying. Open communication and a sense of 'being there' are also important but it is the activities of giving time and listening that he suggests are ultimately crucial. In his critique he identifies 'depersonalisation' rather than death as the ultimate tragedy of life. Key features of 'depersonalisation', he argues, are dying in an alien space, denial of appropriate spiritual nourishment and dying with no hope. Hockey (2002, p. 52) theorises the affirmation of self-identity in terms of acknowledging 'how we have become' as a key biographical spiritual resource that can counter institutional depersonalisation at the end of life. Vivat (2008), reporting findings from a study exploring spiritual caregiving in a hospice in the west of Scotland, makes the further point that we are comprised of 'layers of individual self' (my words) and that spirituality can be conceptualised as what remains when material things drop away and the soul is laid bare. The spiritual part of a person, she argues, lies beneath ego and emotion with spiritual care attending to what goes on deep inside the 'self' of a patient when the ego is stripped away. Vivat (2008) emphasises spiritual caregiving as a highly personal and individual activity but also one that challenges health care workers because of the potential for patient distress. The dominant feature of spiritual care in her study was that of 'accompaniment' characterised by deep and meaningful conversation between a nurse and the patient, stripped of superficiality and 'usual chat' (Vivat, 2008, p. 60). A doctor in this study commenting on the meaning of spiritual care, describes it as 'leading someone to understand themselves' (Vivat, 2008, p. 52), with a further comment from a staff nurse working in the hospice that this was only truly possible when the health worker and the patient are on a 'certain level together' (Vivat, 2008, p. 55).

Kellehear (2005) incorporates the concept of 'depersonalisation' within his model of community care of the dying discussed in Chapter Two. This model is rooted within a public health discourse that positions the dying person as citizen rather than patient. This conceptual shift, he argues, is significant in developing alternative approaches to offering spiritual and other support to the dying. It focuses attention away from specialist professional end-of-life/palliative care giving towards a radically different model that is centred on communities of living rather than on communities or sites of professional caring where patients can be seen to be 'in some sort of custodial relationship with a health care provider' (Kellehear, 2005, p. 47). While palliative care focuses on the whole person as individual, within Kellehear's community model the emphasis is on the whole person as an individual within his or her community. It sees the whole person in full social context in relation to their family, their work, their community involvement and their spiritual beliefs, whatever form these may take. Although Kellehear (2005) does not offer a detailed model of this community approach, he does emphasise the need for wider education of children, young people and adults about death with the aim of promoting understanding on the part of the whole community of its vulnerability and fragility.

At the centre of this alternative approach is the development of non-professional social caring capital that involves friends, family and other kinds of support outside kin relations. The tools of this kind of support include story telling that honours individual and community legacies with 'reflecting back processes' (Kellehear, 2005, p. 63), which are instrumental in maintaining the important spiritual activities of 'reminding' and 'remembering'. A second tool is communication that recognises and privileges reciprocity, with the expectation that dying people will contribute to the spiritual well-being of caregivers and not just be recipients of this type of support. Kellehear's (2005) critique of the development of highly specialised care of the dying calls into question the widely accepted position that the spiritual care needs of dying people have become principally the responsibility of health and social care professionals. In other writing (see Watts, 2008), I have also challenged this assumption, which is explored further below.

Whose job is spiritual care?

Issues of biography and inherited history that contribute to Kellehear's (2005) communitarian model of health promoting palliative care directly challenge a culture of 'depersonalisation' within health care. They also bring to the fore questions about how realistic it is to expect professionals to enter the whole life discourse of the dying person, given the constraints of time and pressure on services that operate within a highly managed system of healthcare such as we have in the UK (Randall and Downie, 2006, p. 154). From the patient's perspective, how is it possible to convey the complexity, richness and diversity of a whole life in small snapshots of rushed time, and are these highly personal disclosures, made to caring professional strangers, of benefit to dying people? Most palliative care literature on this topic assumes that they are. Woods (2007, p. 66) makes the important and related point that palliative care philosophy does not seem to discriminate between a need and a capacity to benefit, resulting in palliative care practitioners feeling obliged to address this element of care for all their patients. Even in hospices, where the patient/staff ratio is higher than in most other care settings, time is still often at a premium for staff, making communication a lower priority than many would wish it to be.

Against this backdrop, from the patients' perspective, the themes of achievement, joy, disappointment, guilt, loss and fear may be deeply held, interwoven and even unsayable, especially as part of the hurried professional encounter. The idea that the psychosocial distress, to which this mix of feelings may contribute, can itself be effectively 'treated' by professionals as they attend the spiritual care needs of the dying is unrealistic, and can lead to a form of 'harassment by questioning in the name of compassion' (Randall and Downie, 2006, p. 153). The pressure on patients to 'disclose' rather than share concerns as part of the patient/professional relationship can result in patients making deeply personal revelations, and feeling unable to dissent from this exchange often because it is part of a wider package of care that is wanted and appreciated.

The time as death approaches may be one for reflection and life review, and for this to be affirming it needs to be shared; for this to offer consistency and congruence to the dying person I suggest that mutuality is also significant. Returning to Chapter Two and the discussion of communication skills, active listening on the part of the health professional is regarded as important and has been emphasised in the palliative care literature. But, in relation to life reflection, as a spiritual activity, what are health professionals listening for in particular? How can they understand or engage with mere fragments of past biography separate from contexts and personalities, when they have known the patient for such a short time? The ability to fit the narrative pieces together so that they cohere as authentic reflection and reconnect people to stories of their past derives from both participants knowing about one another's lives in the context of mutual attachment. This is only truly possible where relationships are longstanding and valued.

In my own research (Watts, 2008) I build on the ideas of Bradshaw (1996), Walter (1997; 2002), Kellehear (2005) and Randall and Downie (2006) to question the relevance of health care workers' involvement with the spiritual well-being of dying people on the basis that spiritual issues are everyday matters that shape our personal histories to make us congruent beings. In my writing I argue that to deeply spiritually connect to another person, there has to be more than compassion and empathy and certainly more than professional duty; there has to be intimacy in the form of mutual knowledge and shared experience. Another term for this deeply held and shared spiritual comfort is love. Use of that term within academic writing does not feel entirely comfortable, given its myriad meanings and manifestations. Nevertheless, it is this term that best captures the intimate and private spiritual exchange that I advocate (Watts, 2008), which might take the form of a mutual reflecting back process of shared remembering or life review.

The concept of love is taken up by Bradshaw (1996) in her critique of what she sees as the gradual secularisation of the spiritual dimension of hospice work. She argues that 'real love' as a manifestation of the Christian ethic of care, has been eroded by a hospice culture of professionalisation in pursuit of a well managed, if not a good death. She argues that without the religious (in this case Christian) dimension, spiritual care work is empty, mechanical work with little benefit for the dying person. She makes the further point that vulnerable, dying people may be at risk of manipulation from this kind of instrumental intervention because of the uneven power relationship inherent in the patient/professional paradigm, a point made similarly by Randall and Downie (2006). Clearly, because her argument adopts a mono-cultural perspective, its relevance to end-of-life care in a multi-cultural society such as we have currently in the UK, must be questioned. Nevertheless, its contention that professionalisation has reduced attempts to address spiritual issues with dying patients to a routine, almost as part of a checklist, is one shared by other commentators.

These ideas may present challenges to health-care professionals supporting dying people as their professional education and training incorporate a remit to include spiritual matters within patient care. The extent to which this remit also recognises the concomitant need on the part of clinicians to have their spiritual needs supported requires investigation and may have policy implications for managers responsible for staff health and safety. Cobb (2008) argues that professionals who work with dying people should be given some form of regular supervision to enable them to explore the impact of intimate personal encounters upon their own spirituality. The aim of supervision is to enable professionals to face their own doubts, fears and prejudices as part of a reflective approach to practice. Although all NHS boards in Scotland have a spiritual care policy, not all of them have chaplains or other dedicated spiritual support workers within hospice or specialist palliative care teams (SPPC, 2007, and see below). That specific discussion aside, we are still left with the question of whose job is it to respond to the spiritual needs of dying people. The answer, as is the case with so many issues connected to death and dying, is not straightforward or absolute and I do not want to suggest another form of prescription or checklist.

As we have seen, dying is an individual experience with its individual and specific features. People die in context and it is this concept of context that is helpful in guiding thinking about who may be the most appropriate spiritual caregivers. I and others have argued for spiritual care-taking of dying people to be a personal and intimate exchange based on longstanding and valued relationships, such as may exist between spouses, partners, family members, friends and ministers of faith (see Watts, 2008). Some people, however, may not be part of positive close networks and for some, whose connections to family and friends have been negatively affected by conflict, distance and differing lifestyles, the opportunity to 'remember together' may be very limited. In these circumstances, the importance of the availability of a caring professional stranger (as contextual newcomer), to provide spiritual support, should be acknowledged. Wright (2004) notes that this can be a difficult area of practice, precisely because everyone is an individual, and also because the concept of spirituality is so diffuse, as the discussion above has demonstrated. This diffuseness, however, he argues, may offer opportunities for health-care workers to make different kinds of spiritual connections with patients on a number of levels.

Not all dying people want to engage in life review or discuss their spiritual beliefs and this, too, needs to be acknowledged and respected. Just sitting in silence, holding a patient's hand or giving them their mouth rinse may be spiritually meaningful. As a final thought on this topic, despite the growing secularisation of UK society, we should not lose sight of the relevance for many people of religious faith of receiving support in their dying from religious leaders, as part of a lived spiritual continuum. Cobb (2001) argues that in the context of death and dying it is difficult within the UK to avoid aspects of the sacred and dimensions of religion which are embedded within the various cultures that contribute to a multi-faith society. There has thus developed within many hospitals and hospices the phenomenon of multi-faith chaplaincy, which can respond to local 'faith conditions' to try to ensure that appropriate religious spiritual support is available to those who want it. Hodgson *et al.* (2009, p. 107) characterise the essence of a chaplain's role as that of being fully present in relation to the emotional and spiritual realties of life's crises and transitions. Mayne (2006), an Anglican priest, writing about his own impending death from cancer, draws on a broad Christian chaplaincy to sustain his faith, which he describes as being 'firm ground'. Much writing on this topic connects religious faith with certainty about the future for those facing death and Mayne (2006) characterises this as healing. He makes the further point that, although religious belief in whatever form is ordered by precepts and prescription, it is experienced individually at a deeply personal level and this can be nurtured by ministers of faith, even in the impersonal setting of the hospital, with the result that patients are reassured and their integrity and worth maintained.

Spiritual care policy in Scotland

In recent years there have been substantial changes in approaches to spiritual care in Scotland. This activity is now understood to involve all NHS workers, with attention to cultural competence and the respect for individuals the underpinning core values of both policy and practice. Hay (2002), writing about contemporary spirituality in the context of Scottish health care, emphasises how important it is for care workers to acknowledge both individuality and diversity in addressing the spiritual needs of those who are sick or dying. This change has taken place against a background of the drive for increased efficiency in health service delivery within a rationalised business model characterised by targets and audit, making it increasingly difficult for staff to fully attend to the whole-person needs of their patients (Elliot, 2002).

Current NHS policy on spiritual care in Scotland is based on extensive consultation with both faith communities and secular interest groups such as the Humanist Society of Scotland and has drawn heavily on the findings from the Working Party on Chaplaincy and Spiritual Care set up by the Scottish Executive Health Department (SEHD, 2000). The Working Party was established to consider new guidelines for the delivery of spiritual care in the light of changes to patterns of religious belief, a stronger emphasis on care in the community and changes to chaplaincy with the growth of professionalism and increased demands on chaplains to minister to patients, staff and family members. The cardinal principle of impartiality was invoked to ensure respect for a wide range of beliefs, lifestyles and cultures with services characterised by openness, sensitivity, integrity and compassion. Thus, while religious spiritual care is offered within the context of shared beliefs, NHS policy is that other forms of spiritual care should be person-centred without judgements or assumptions. As discussed above, the fundamental core values of self-worth, relationships and life review contribute to approaches to broader spiritual care that is focused on holism. The appointment and employment of chaplains is the responsibility of NHS Boards and this work is centrally funded. Under the aegis and supervision of these Boards each faith community is able to appoint its own chaplain or spiritual caregiver to ensure pastoral and doctrinal suitability for the community they serve.

There is, however, a paradox emerging with, on the one hand, emphasis on individual health care workers taking responsibility for the spiritual care of patients and, on the other, the policy imperative to employ professional chaplains with dedicated expertise. Each Board is able to determine the detail of its own spiritual care provision and some see it as the role of the chaplaincy service to contribute to the training and professional development of health care staff to make them better equipped to recognise spiritual need in their patients, make referrals and offer spiritual care themselves (McGregor, 2002). Other tensions relate to the feasibility of offering sensitive one-to-one spiritual care amidst the busy professional culture of a modern hospital where opportunities for staff to talk and listen to patients are increasingly scarce. Elliot (2002) suggests that the rise of new integrative approaches to health and well-being, with their greater emphasis on spirituality and complementary therapies, may in part be due to the more intimate person-to-person nature of alternative therapeutic encounters in contrast to rushed exchanges in busy clinical environments. Ryan (2002), writing about spiritual care in the context of the Scottish health care system, goes further, suggesting that there has been a relocation of the ideal health care relationship out of mainstream health care into the complementary sector. Whether spiritual care-giving within the context of health will gradually become the province of independent practitioners remains to be seen, but the challenge to policy makers to retain a role for spiritual care-giving within mainstream provision may increasingly be a function of evaluation based on the paradigmatic imperatives of 'value-for-money' and evidence-based practice.

Summary

This chapter has highlighted the increase in the West of secular forms of spirituality that privilege ideas of interconnectedness (Thorne, 2005) and the valuing of our relationships to one another rather than our relationship to God or other 'higher being'. Holloway (2007) emphasises the significance of spirituality in affecting bereavement and calls for more research in this area. She argues that relationships and notions of relatedness strongly influence the individual experience of bereavement, which is shaped by social and cultural context. These issues are now explored in the next chapter, which considers social and psychological theories of grief, while the issues facing practitioners working to support bereaved people are taken up in Chapter Six.

CHAPTER 5

Understanding Grief

Grief, as a social and psychological phenomenon, has been the subject of extensive study which, until fairly recently, has been dominated by behavioural scientific approaches within the domains of psychiatry and psychology (Howarth, 2007). For many, the death of a loved one is very traumatic with multi-dimensional effects that can be broadly understood as a deep and irrevocable disruption to 'normal' life. For practitioners who are helping bereaved people to make transitions through the experience of loss, it is important to understand some of the body of theory that has been developed to explain different types of grief reaction. However, such understanding should always be framed by an appreciation that no two bereavements are the same and also that those working in bereavement support roles will bring their own interpretations and subjectivities to the support encounter.

Attempts to understand human emotions and behaviour involve looking for patterns and themes. The work of developing models of grief, though criticised by some on the basis of their potential to 'normalise' grief behaviours, has the positive aim of comforting those who grieve by reassuring them that their responses are natural and are shared by others. No matter where in the life course a death occurs, it is often hard for those who survive to adjust and although Leming and Dickinson (2007, p. 519) claim that 'experiencing the death of someone else is a growth experience', this may not be the way those who are suffering bereavement see the experience, at least not for some time. Indeed, for some bereaved people, attempts to rationalise what is always a uniquely individual and often highly emotional experience (despite the universality of death itself), can be seen at best as reductionist and, at worst, insulting. It is thus important to acknowledge at the outset that some bereaved people are resistant to having their grief categorised, compared or explained because they see this as an attempt to make their grief something to be 'regulated' rather than valued as an intense emotion of loss, and practitioners should be aware of this possibility.

It was the psychiatrist Erich Lindemann (1944) who first discussed the concepts of 'normal' and 'abnormal' grief. 'Normal' grief, he argued, would run a natural course and resolve itself whereas 'abnormal' grief might require some form of clinical intervention or structured support as a form of professional care of the bereaved, with this potentially positioning some grief as illness (Currer, 2001). The extent to which the bereaved person 'lets go' or 'holds on' to the deceased person, in an emotional sense, is central to the 'normal'/'abnormal' continuum. Other considerations are the timeframe of grief and its impact on a person's ability to perform daily activities. The concepts of 'letting go' and 'holding on' to the dead person contribute to most theories of grief and these are revisited in the discussion of the principal theories set out below.

Grief is first and foremost an experience of loss, where former certainties or expectations are replaced by uncertainty and disorientation, and this chapter will begin with a discussion of loss as generic concept. This will be followed by consideration of different theories of grief that have been developed in modern Western societies, exploring these from both a psychological and social perspective, and highlighting those that have been most influential in guiding approaches to bereavement care, which forms the theme of Chapter Six.

Exploring loss

In the context of bereavement Weinstein (2008, p. 2) offers a working definition of loss characterising it as 'wider than a response to a death, important as that is. It is any separation from someone or something whose significance is such that it impacts on our physical or emotional well-being, role and status'. He develops this definition by adding that the experience and manifestation of loss can be more or less difficult depending on other important variables. The first of these variables relates to the different meanings or 'types' of death.

Biological death within medical terminology is when the body expires and there is cessation of all function.

Social death occurs when someone may be in a coma, in a permanent vegetative state, or suffering from advanced stages of dementia. Individuals may be alive in the biological sense but cut off from former social links. Weinstein (2008) includes prisoners in this category and Sandman (2005) refers to the loss of role as a further form of social death. Lawton (2000) argues that this loss of role for those approaching death may be just as significant as the experience of physical deterioration and is characterised by changed relationships.

Psychosocial death is when someone's psychological essence or prior sense of self is perceived to have died (Weinstein, 2008). This may be through drug dependency, joining a cult or through some forms of mental illness.

Added to the above, definition of the terms bereavement, grief and mourning is necessary to theoretically situate the discussion of the grief models that are the principal theme of this chapter. *Bereavement* is the response to loss and has been present in all cultures through history. *Grief* is the emotional and psychological expression of bereavement and can be characterised by intense sorrow. Grief is multi-faceted with physical, cognitive, behavioural and social dimensions. Parkes (2000, p. 326) explains that 'grief is essentially an emotion that draws us toward something or someone that is missing'. *Mourning,* as the social expression of grief, is culturally determined. In some traditions mourning has a distinct temporal dimension; in the Jewish faith, for example, there is a prescribed period of mourning during which the bereaved are supported in their expression of grief with a view to their integrating the loss and moving forward in their lives (Golbert, 2006).

The above set of categorisations and definitions is useful in pointing to the different kinds of loss and behavioural responses associated with the broad concept of death. The way that loss is experienced when someone dies will also be influenced by a number of social and circumstantial factors such as the nature of the attachment and relationship with the dead person, whether the death was sudden or anticipated, whether the death was traumatic, religious beliefs, complications arising from the death such as loss of home or income, and the kind of support available to the bereaved person.

The ideas of Bowlby (1991) in relation to his theory of attachment have been widely drawn on to develop understanding of the ways in which losses of different kinds may or may not be significant. His psychological theory, which draws on the work of Freud (1984), is based on the assumption that human beings have an innate drive to form attachments to significant people. This starts in infancy with the first primary attachment, usually made with parents, which enables children to explore with confidence connections to other people and return (in the emotional sense) to the primary caregiver. This early attachment is thought to provide a sense of security and safety, and responses to being separated from the primary caregiver include despair, protest and yearning.

In considering adult responses to loss, Bowlby argues that our earliest attachments are significant in influencing how in adulthood we negotiate relationships, establish independence and cope with different kinds of loss in our lives. In infancy, retaining a sense of the principal caregiver (often the mother) as internalised object stored in the memory, strengthens identity when separated from the caregiver. This pattern, Bowlby argues, may be repeated in adulthood in respect of the death of someone significant. When separated from someone through death a range of responses may result that often involve disorientation and deep distress. The desire to have the deceased person back conflicts with reality and it is this conflict that is at the root of what Bowlby terms 'separation anxiety', which can involve fear of being without the dead person, disrupted sleep and nightmares about the separation.

The value of Bowlby's attachment theory has been recognised in other 'loss contexts' such as divorce, unemployment and loss of identity and status resulting from conflict and migration. These losses can challenge the way we see ourselves and the world, as well as threatening the 'taken for granted' assumptions that underpin our daily lives and structure our thoughts, expectations and feelings. The significance of assumptions in influencing responses to loss is taken up by Parkes (1988) in his model of psychosocial transitions.

Psychosocial transitions and 'assumptive worlds'

Parkes (2000) argues that the life events that have the greatest potential to destabilise us are those that require us to make major changes to the assumptions that frame our daily lives; these events are likely to have lasting implications and usually occur over a short time period affording little opportunity for preparation. Events such as these are termed psychosocial transitions; they initiate the need to change our internal world in respect of expectations and assumptions that are based on everything that we assume to be true about our lives. The death, for example, of a spouse or other close relative may invalidate assumptions about all aspects of our lives. Habits, routines and patterns predicated on the assumption of the presence and role of the deceased person have to be revised and adapted in the light of the changed reality.

Change can be difficult and painful because so much behaviour that frames the ebb and flow of life is almost instinctive and automatic with daily rituals enacted routinely. We may, for example, prepare supper for seven o'clock on Mondays because our partner needs to be out by eight to attend an evening class and when the partner is gone our sense of this structure is destroyed. This is one small example but where the deceased person was our carer or the main income earner in the household adaptation can be difficult both on a psychological and a practical level. Grief can serve to 'disorganise' our lives making us feel insecure and vulnerable. The responses to this profound life change can take many forms. Parkes (2000) refers to a range of behaviours including withdrawal from the world to avoid being confronted by others as they react to our changed circumstances. He cites avoidance and distracting activities as one way of not fully acknowledging what has happened. Whatever the behavioural response of the bereaved person, it will be necessary for them to relearn their assumptive world and reassemble a different set of assumptions to underpin their everyday life. In this task they may be suffering from separation anxiety and feel helpless and emotionally and practically incompetent.

As part of this model, Parkes (2000) acknowledges the importance of different kinds of support in helping the bereaved person to make appropriate changes. He states that 'three things are needed: emotional support, protection through the period of helplessness and assistance in discovering new models of the world appropriate to the emergent situation' (Parkes, 2000, p. 329). This support is aimed at helping the bereaved person make the successful transition from one assumptive world to another. The different approaches to bereavement care are considered in the next chapter. However it is relevant to make the point here that disentangling attachment theory from transition theory, in striving for a better understanding of grief responses in order to offer the most appropriate support, can be challenging. Given the additional impact of cultural and wider social factors, supporting those who find themselves in transition can be a complex and long-term task.

The tasks of mourning

Drawing on psychological theory and interviews with bereaved people, William Worden (1982) developed his model known as the '*four tasks of mourning*'. This model is comprised of four tasks or stages and is intended to be of use to practitioners in their support of bereaved people, particularly in pursuit of 'healthy' outcomes whereby grief does not become complicated, hindering growth and development. The four tasks are outlined below; these can be understood as 'grief work' on the part of the bereaved and they do not necessarily flow in sequence, with some tasks being revisited during this process.

> **Task 1** Accepting the reality of the loss – this involves accepting that the person is dead and will not return. Such acceptance must be at both an intellectual and emotional level and some mourning rituals, such as the funeral, can help the bereaved to accept the reality of the death.

Task 2 Experience and work through the pain of grief – the pain of grief will vary from individual to individual. For some it will take the form of anger and may be experienced as very intense; attempts to avoid the experience of feeling this pain may result in the onset of depression later.

Task 3 Adjusting to an environment in which the dead person is missing – this adjustment will depend on a number of factors, principally the relationship with the deceased and the role the deceased person had in the life of the bereaved person. During this task, the emphasis is on coming to terms with the absence of the deceased person on all levels, practical, emotional and sensory, and it is important that the bereaved person does not fall into a state of helplessness. This aspect of grief work also involves starting to make sense of the loss as a way of regaining control over his or her life.

Task 4 Relocating the deceased emotionally and moving on – at this stage the bereaved finds the ability to emotionally invest in something or someone else. Letting go means finding an appropriate place for the deceased in their emotional life; memories of the deceased are not forgotten but are shared. With time the mourner is able to redefine him or herself.

Worden's model has been widely adopted by bereavement counsellors, who have seen it as a useful tool with which to support the bereaved in experiencing a healthy grieving process. This will be referred to in more detail in the next chapter. Despite this, Worden's task approach has not been without its critics (see Walter, 1999, for example), who claim that it is prescriptive with its emphasis directed towards the ways in which the bereaved *should* grieve. Such prescription, it is argued, may also entail little scope for cultural flexibility.

Elisabeth Kubler-Ross and the stages of grief

Kubler-Ross's (1970) stages of grief model has been widely referred to in the literature and now constitutes a familiar approach to bereavement support. Like Worden's model, it is comprised of a number of stages or phases. It is, however, important to state that this model of grief has been adapted from Kubler-Ross's research with dying patients in the Chicago hospital where she worked as a doctor. Her research was aimed at exploring how terminally ill patients approach their death, specifically she explains that 'we would observe critically ill patients, study their responses and needs, evaluate the reactions of the people around them, and get as close to the dying as they would allow us' (Kubler-Ross, 1970, p. 19). From this work she developed a five-stage model of the attitudes of those who are facing their own death.

> *Denial* – This first stage can best be summed up as 'It can't be true: there must be some mistake'. Denial can function as a buffer after unexpected shocking news but it can leave the dying person isolated.

> *Anger* – When the first stage of denial and unreality cannot be maintained any longer, feelings of anger and resentment set in, with the question of 'why me?' a common response. Anger may be directed at family and friends as well as at clinical staff. The prospect of death may be experienced as a cruel and untimely injustice.

> *Bargaining* – This third stage, whereby the dying person attempts to strike a deal with fate as a way of trying to postpone the inevitable, may only be present for a brief period. Sometimes the bargaining may be linked to a particular family event such as a wedding or birth of a grandchild.

> *Depression* – When the terminally ill patient can no longer deny his illness and is suffering increased pain and weakness, his anger and rage will be replaced by a sense of loss experienced by many as a deep depression.

> *Acceptance* – The final stage in this model is characterised by the dying patient starting to let go of life as a way of beginning to accept their impending death. This may not be an entirely calm state but is likely to be one of resigned expectation.

Because grief has come to be understood as a process with different phases, Kubler-Ross's five-stage model of dying has been seen as an appropriate theoretical tool in respect of grief and bereavement. Counsellors and other professionals have seen the usefulness of this and other models that continue to influence practice in this area. There are, however, problems associated with their use, particularly in relation to their interpretation as prescriptive rather than descriptive, discussed in relation to Worden's task approach. The reality that for many, grief comes and goes in its intensity, almost in 'waves', with good and bad days, is not properly reflected in stage theory. Additionally, with the Kubler-Ross model, the sense that a sequence of responses is expected with each stage being completed before the next can be seen as particularly rigid and inflexible. For those who may not experience each of these stages, this can have the effect of making them feel that they are 'incompetent' or 'inadequate' grievers. It also fails to acknowledge that people may oscillate between stages and that in some cases (for example, parents' grief at the loss of a child, the 'ultimate theft' (Harman, 1981; also see Grinyer, 2002)) acceptance, as 'moving on', may be unrealistic.

The dual process model

Margaret Stroebe and Henk Schut (1999; Stroebe *et* al., 2005) offer what they claim is a less prescriptive model of grief that focuses on coping processes. Their concept, of oscillation between different kinds of coping behaviours, has two orientations. The first focuses on the loss of the deceased (loss orientation) and the second (restoration orientation) aims to avoid dwelling on the loss as a means of starting to make adjustments for the future. They argue that both orientations are necessary to adjust to the loss and move on but that the bereaved may move across these at different times and with varying intensity. This 'forwards and backwards' or 'switching' approach to explaining grief acknowledges the importance of culture, gender, age and the individual circumstances of the death. The model also incorporates the idea that the bereaved may be emotionally overwhelmed by the pain of grief and that 'taking time out' from their grief may help them make the necessary adjustments to enable them to rebuild their lives.

Thompson (1997), commenting on this model, draws out its flexibility in relation to issues of social difference such as gender. He observes that a loss orientation may be seen as a characteristically female approach in contrast to the restoration orientation associated with more masculine approaches that focus on activities and 'doing' rather than feeling. He commends the model to practitioners because of its ongoing dialectic feature that obviates the more common 'either/or' approach. He also notes that the dual process model successfully accounts for the notion that some people never completely get over their loss, so that although the loss orientation is submerged it may re-surface at poignant times and is never eliminated altogether. In non-theoretical language this seems to be saying 'living with the loss but not getting over it is OK'.

Social and cultural models of loss and grief

Dissatisfaction with psychologically based theories has led to the develop-ment of a plethora of alternative social and cultural theories of loss and grief broadly arguing that human grief is socially distributed and socially patterned (Prior, 2000). The work of Peter Marris (1974), which draws heavily on sociological explanations, has been influential. His model addresses wider issues of loss (such as those connected to slum clearance and forced unemployment) not just those associated with death. He asserts that loss and change are inextricably linked and that there is a natural human impulse towards conservatism that is more comfortable with predictability and is resistant to change. For him, as with Bowlby, the key period is childhood when meanings about the people and circumstances of life are formed, then carried into adulthood when they are difficult to revise. Marris (1974, p. 4) calls these familiar and predictable patterns of understanding 'structures of meaning' and argues that many experiencing loss will hold fast to these as a way of holding on to their former reality.

Other social theorists have contributed different perspectives about ways in which grief and bereavement can be understood. Walter (1996; 1999) has been influential in this area, particularly with his postmodern model which links bereavement to biography, arguing that the purpose of grief is 'the construc-tion of a durable biography that enables the living to integrate the memory of the dead into their ongoing lives' (1996, p. 7). Central to this model is not the 'abandonment' of the deceased from the life and consciousness of the bereaved but their continuing presence, made secure by the sharing of memories between the bereaved person and those who knew the deceased. This involves talking about the deceased to confirm their identity as part of a continuing biography and also to maintain their ongoing membership of the family and community. The position of the deceased as guide, role model, caretaker of the values of the bereaved and as honoured ancestor is sustained through the exchange of stories. Walter (1999) extends this theme of the continuity of the dead in the lives of the bereaved with reference to the bereaved talking to the dead. He argues that such talk can serve several functions, including helping the bereaved resolve issues of identity as well as maintaining the ongoing presence of the dead person within their emotional life as a form of support. He describes these behaviours that connect the living with the dead as private bonds because these 'conversations' generally take place without others being present.

This model connects well with the work of Klass *et al.* (1996) who suggest that 'successful' grieving is dependent upon the bereaved finding ways of continuing the bonds with their dead loved one so that the relationship between the living and the dead can be maintained. This suggests that the dead should not be forgotten or abandoned but should be reincorporated into the lives of the living. This theory may give rise to tensions between 'letting the dead go' and the bereaved moving forward and the bereaved 'holding on' to dead loved ones in a way that may hinder them from adapting to life without the physical presence of the deceased person. Interestingly, Parkes (1988) situates the continuing bonds thesis within psychosocial transitions theory noting that this model is not radically different from others before it. Howarth (2007, p. 209) makes the further observation that 'continuing bonds may reflect a proclivity in contemporary Western societies to blur the boundaries between the living and the dead'.

The essence of both Walter's (1999) and Klass *et al.*'s (1996) theoretical approaches can be summed up by the phrase 'remembering not dismembering', with Howarth (2007) suggesting that biographical reconstruction of the dead person is now seen by many as a new orthodoxy of grief. This does run counter to early dominant understandings about resolved grief or closure, with these outcomes, framed by powerful medical discourses of health and pathology, thought to be dependent on the bereaved letting the deceased go and breaking the bonds.

Disenfranchised grief

As this text is aimed at a wide range of practitioners across the health and social care sector, the omission of the concept 'disenfranchised grief' would be a serious error. As with other behaviours connected to death and dying, grief is socially constructed with social scripts provided to grievers from others in the community who recognise their grief as appropriate. The grief theories outlined above, therefore, all involve some kind of social recognition that the deceased person is valued by the bereaved and that the death is significant in some way in changing the life of the bereaved person. The work of Kenneth Doka (1989; 2002) has been instrumental in developing understandings about the ways in which some grief may not be socially acknowledged or sanctioned or not regarded as genuine. His model of disenfranchised grief includes unrecognised relationships, unrecognised losses and unrecognised grievers, and these categories are all characterised by the underlying feature of stigma or invisibility attached to the loss.

Unrecognised relationships may be those that are outside family ties, such as friends or neighbours; a partner in a gay or lesbian relationship; relationships that are focused on the past such as ex-spouses; extramarital attachments that are hidden; professional caregivers who have formed attachments to the deceased; birth parents of adopted children.

Unrecognised losses include: death of a pet seen as 'just an animal' so invoking ridicule; birth mothers who give up their child for adoption; perinatal death, in particular death during pregnancy; abortions, because even though the dominant reaction of women having a termination is one of relief, others who have a pregnancy terminated due to fetal abnormality may experience profound grief at the death of their child; the return of foster children to their birth parents; social death, for example with Alzheimer's disease where a family member, though alive, may be perceived as 'dead'; death from AIDS where the deceased is regarded as being culpable; death from a drug overdose that is seen to involve an element of choice or poor decision-making.

Unrecognised grievers include: people with learning difficulties who may be thought incapable of understanding or processing the loss; children who may be perceived as too young to understand (the grief of children will be a discussion topic in the next chapter); those who are seen as too old, as might be the case in residents of a care home.

Because of the lack of social recognition, disenfranchised grief is a hidden grief that is often experienced in isolation with no framework for its legitimate expression and this can have the effect of increasing the reaction to the loss. Being excluded from mourning rituals may intensify feelings of powerlessness and may lead to suppressed or delayed grief reactions. In some cases disenfranchised grief may lie dormant for years because the opportunity or 'proper time' for its expression does not materialise. Such a delay can also be caused by fear of hostile reactions to its expression and this delay may lead to the development of chronic unresolved grief that can grow in intensity over time. Added to these emotional difficulties there may in some cases be further practical and legal complications connected to inheritance and property rights.

Clearly, because disenfranchised grief derives from a loss for which there is no socially recognised right or role to grieve, the provision of sensitive support is challenging. Offering different support formats so that the bereaved person has a choice about how they share their loss is one way that professionals can respond. Weinstein (2008) highlights the importance of listening on the part of those supporting bereaved people who may have 'invisible' grief. He suggests that this will allow them to give voice to their loss and express 'disallowed' feelings.

Anticipatory grief

The discussion so far has concentrated on exploring understandings of post-death grief and bereavement. Grief, as the expression of loss, may, however, be present pre-death and can be experienced by the dying person as well as those close to him who anticipate the death. Specifically, anticipatory grief, first developed as a concept by Lindemann (1944), can occur when there is an opportunity to anticipate death. Research on anticipatory grief, much of which has centred on whether grieving before the event of death can lessen the burden and intensity of grief after death, has been contradictory and problematic. Some studies have found that anticipated loss results in an easier grief experience while others report no significant difference. It is difficult to assess the evidence, particularly as there is a range of other personal and social factors that can influence the experience of grief, with expected or unexpected loss just one feature of the death. These factors include the cause of death, family circumstances, the nature and meaning of the person and relationship to be lost and the personal characteristics of the griever.

This form of grief has been shown to be multi-faceted with temporal dimensions. The death of someone close may be a final loss but there can be many losses experienced before death, such as loss of the future, reduced levels of functioning and the necessary abandonment of projects. Rando (1986, p. 13), commenting on the multi-faceted nature of this phenomenon, points to 'losses of things past, losses in the present and losses that will occur in the future' as elements of anticipatory grief. Looked at in these terms, anticipatory grief involves a series of grieving episodes and those experiencing such grief may need comfort and support before as well as after the death. This may especially be the case for informal caregivers who have close involvement in looking after the dying person. They may be suffering from care-related stress and Bass and Bowman (1990) argue that they may need support to maintain social connections, as these may be instrumental in helping them make post-death adjustments.

Summary

In this chapter I have sought to provide a description of what I see as the main grief theories contained in the literature. I have not presented these within discrete psychological or non-psychological categories because some theories (for example, Stroebe and Schut's (1999) dual process model) incorporate both social and psychological dimensions. The models I have chosen to include reflect a range of contrasting and complementary approaches but they do not comprise a fully comprehensive coverage of either past or contemporary theories. The literature on grief and bereavement is vast and growing and this area of enquiry is seen as one ripe for research. Those working as bereavement counsellors may well draw on a range of theories to develop a strategy for understanding a particular grief and for providing appropriately sensitive bereavement care, applying different models in different circumstances. This is in part because all grief is first and foremost individual; no two situations are the same and often it is the social context of the bereavement that is crucial in affecting the experience of grief. The importance of the place of the family in the grief dynamic has been little touched upon here but this, too, can be the source of tension as family members respond to their loss in different ways.

The understanding of grief as both an individual and social phenomenon has been at the root of much contemporary theorising that challenges notions of there being an essentialist or universal way of managing loss. In the light of this Weinstein (2008, p. 42) suggests that 'it is for each individual to find their own meaning and construct their own narrative'. Despite the growing dominance of individualist approaches, a theme common across most models of grief is that the bereaved need to face up to their loss to enable them to reshape their lives. Although it is now widely recognised that grief reactions can vary in their length and disruptive effects, with consequent notions of 'good' and 'bad' grieving being highly subjective and culturally determined, this is not to say that all bereaved people will need help to adjust to their changed life. Those involved in bereavement support work, however, do need some theoretical models to inform a knowledge base for their practice, even if these models are increasingly being regarded as a 'guide' rather than a 'template' for effective practice. The extent to which the subjective views and values of bereavement workers shape the support they provide will vary from one practitioner to another. This concern, together with a range of other practical considerations such as organisational development and training, is among the topics discussed in the next chapter.

CHAPTER 6

Supporting Bereaved People

It is acknowledged that grief, as a response to a significant loss, has a marked effect on mortality and morbidity and that some bereaved people are at risk of suffering psychological distress as they adjust to life without the deceased person. Mor *et al.* (1986) found that when age, sex and prior health were controlled for, bereaved spouses were at increased risk of visits to and from doctors, admission to hospital, use of medication to control anxiety and increased consumption of alcohol, compared with the national average. These effects will result in the need for care and support during bereavement, and this chapter considers a range of approaches to supporting bereaved people with a separate focus on the particular needs of children and young people.

Bereavement care comes in many forms, draws on different social and psychological grief models (see Chapter Five) and is available in a wide range of both clinical and voluntary settings. Most bereavement care is character-ised by mainly professionalised and 'expert' approaches, as part of a burgeon-ing 'death industry' as discussed in Chapter One. In his critique of the social context of bereavement in modern Western societies, Walter (1999) argues that, because the experience of grief has become essentially private with social mourning now generally abandoned, uncertainty about the 'normality' of feelings of grief and sadness has led to the development of professional skills and services aimed principally at providing reassurance to the bereaved person. We now see sessions on bereavement included as part of the training of doctors, nurses, social workers, police officers and ministers of religion with an emphasis on recognising and responding to the needs of the bereaved person as an individual. In parallel, however, individual grief behaviours have become theorised and are subject to categorisation such as 'process', 'recovery' and 'resolution' and are 'regulated through these categories and through the possibility of expert counselling and mutual help groups' (Walter, 1999, p. 187). The medicalisation of grief, constructed as an illness requiring treatment so as to minimise psychological or even physical harm, has still not quite disappeared and Walter (1999, p. 187) notes that 'the main professional help available is pills from the doctor'.

While some social and practical support for bereaved people will come from informal networks such as family, friends and neighbours, the dispersed and increasingly complex patterns of kinship relations suggest that continuity of this type of informal support, particularly over an extended period, may not be realistic and there now exists a range of services dedicated to providing bereavement care. The two most common forms of help are one-to-one counselling and mutual help groups (Walter, 1999) and these are now discussed below focusing on both theoretical and practical/organisational aspects.

Counselling

In recent decades counselling and therapy have expanded enormously as a panacea for all kinds of difficult experiences and behaviours that include relationship breakdown, debt problems, sexual dysfunction and psychiatric conditions. Within the UK counselling has emerged as central to the way that death and grief is managed and now has a highly developed practice domain within a strong institutional framework (Arnason, 2001). Seale (1998, p. 196) states that bereavement counselling, as psychological intervention, has the twin purpose of restoring ontological security and promoting social cohesion. He expands this point explaining that 'counselling is a type of performative ritual in which people are offered the opportunity to write themselves into a dominant cultural script, resulting in the reward of secure membership of an imagined community' (Seale, 1998, p. 196).

Seale's (1998) ideas are highly sophisticated and provide a useful starting point from which to explore both the theory and practice of counselling as one approach to supporting bereaved people; however, the concepts 'ontological security' and 'social cohesion' require clarification. Giddens's (1991) concept of ontological security derives from a sense of continuity with regard to an individual's life events. It is framed by a sense of order with which people are able to give meaning to their lives. To be ontologically secure is to possess understanding of one's place in the world and is a prerequisite for the competence of self-worth and self-identity that Giddens argues is not simply given, but must be routinely created, renewed and sustained in the activities of the individual. This understanding of 'self' is therefore a narrative that establishes the continuity of an individual's existence as him or herself and has relational value; in other words we are who we are by virtue of our biographical history that involves both roles and relationships with others. In the context of bereavement, the term social cohesion can best be understood with reference to the ideas of both Parkes (2000) and Stroebe and Schut (1999) discussed in the previous chapter. Developing a revised assumptive world, as described by Parkes (2000), contributes to a new social structure framed by a restoration orientation (Stroebe and Schut, 1999) that aims to avoid dwelling on the loss as a means of starting to make adjustments for the future in light of a new social reality.

Weinstein (2008), writing principally to inform social work practice in the area of loss, death and bereavement, adds to Seale's (1998) ideas about the aims of bereavement counselling. He identifies the following aims:

- supporting the grieving and mourning process;
- encouraging the expression of grief, sadness, anger, anxiety, hopelessness, helplessness, despair;
- reviewing both the positive and negative aspects of the lost relationship;
- working through old unresolved losses;
- giving reassurances about the normality of the psychological aspects of grief;
- giving the mourner space to take stock of their new situation, which may include taking new directions;
- allowing the mourner to gain a fuller and enduring sense of the deceased.

A number of the above features were evident in the counselling support I received following the sudden death of my father on his way to work. I was 23 at the time and just beginning to establish myself as an independent adult in the world. His death left me completely devastated and I felt for a long time that I had lost my 'footing' in the world, being no longer a daughter to anyone (see Watts, 2009a). I can recall that much of the exchange I had with the counsellor was dominated by feelings of anger that he had died and left me (my mother having died when I was eight) and by an unstoppable urge on my part to talk about him, encouraged by the counsellor, who on more than one occasion said simply 'tell me about him'. I remember recounting his love of cricket, his sense of fun, his dislike of work, his hopes for retirement and his love of me. I suppose what I was creating in the counselling encounter was a biographical snapshot of my father and, in so doing, was 'holding on' to him as a continuing material reality in my life.

The person-centred therapeutic approach formulated by Carl Rogers (1951) is widely used in bereavement counselling and Bryant-Jefferies (2006), using a case study model, provides an authoritative account of how this approach works in practice. Some of the key points he outlines are now presented in general terms to give the reader an overview of person-centred theoretical principles and their application to practice. A number of core 'conditions' underpin a person-centred approach as follows:

- two people in psychological contact;
- one (the client) is vulnerable and anxious;
- the other (the counsellor) is congruent and committed to the relationship with the client;
- the counsellor has unconditional positive regard for the client;
- the counsellor has an empathic understanding of the beliefs and inner world of the client and endeavours to communicate this empathic understanding to the client.

These conditions frame a particular type of therapeutic dialogue as a central component of this form of counselling that may not necessarily take place in a face-to-face context but can be transacted over the phone or even across the internet (Bryant-Jefferies, 2006). It is important for the counsellor to have an empathic approach as this enables them to enter the private perceptual world of the client in a sensitive manner; this helps develop rapport and trust, which can be a delicate process. Much has been written about the meaning and represent-ation of 'unconditional positive regard'; for the current purpose this can be explained as a warm acceptance by the counsellor of the way the client is and of what the client discloses. This is not the same as 'agreeing with' what the client says but is a form of valuing in the moment the humanity of the client in a non-judgemental way. Reference to the congruent and committed stance of the counsellor refers to authenticity or genuineness in their attitudes and feelings about the client. In summary, Bryant-Jefferies (2006) argues that effective counselling practice is based on the development by counsellors of a facilita-tive relationship with their clients and requires of them the skills of disciplined listening, use of accessible 'non-technical' language, sensitivity and gentleness, allowing the client to take the lead and establish the pace of the session. Empathy should be expressed in body language as well as verbal behaviour. A further skill is that of silence, and the impact of this can be very profound for the client, particularly in enabling them to see the gains they make as a consequence of both their expression and reflection (Weinstein, 2008).

Grief can be 'messy' (Arnason, 2001, p. 129) and each grief is unique which means that it is likely to involve some measure of unpredictability. Clients may attend counselling for bereavement at very different stages in the process of coming to terms with their experience and adjusting to the new social reality of their lives (Seale, 1998). Furthermore, they may not proactively seek this kind of support but take this up on the basis of referral by their doctor or other health or social care worker. Bereavement is two-directional, with a dual focus on what is lost by the absence of the deceased person and also on the loss of the future that would have involved that person. For some people one aspect may be more important than the other and in the case, for instance, of the death of a child, it is the loss for parents of an expected future involving both the child and the family dynamic incorporating the child (Riches and Dawson, 2000) that may be paramount. The work of helping clients explore, express and understand their emotions (Arnason, 2001, p. 125) is demanding, and recognition of this is reflected in the level of training and professionalism that now attaches to the bereavement counsellor role. Some of this will be considered further as part of the critique of the bereavement support organisation Cruse that follows later in this chapter.

Mutual help groups

These groups come in a variety of forms and may be informally as well as formally constituted but their unifying feature is that they represent a specific community of experience. For example, in the USA there is a 9/11 survivors group following the September 11th attacks on New York; in the UK disasters in the 1980s and 1990s, such as Lockerbie and Hillsborough, led to the establishment of mutual support groups for bereaved families and friends of those who died. Such groups enable members to tell their stories and express their feelings to each other in a way that may not be possible or seen as 'legitimate' outside the group or in other settings. Walter (1999, p. 187) describes these groups as 'fictive kinship groups' whose members become bonded through shared trauma. Walter (1999) describes how a leading figure in the Lockerbie support group had found professional counsellors to be of no use, with only the support from other Lockerbie members proving helpful. Other groups come into being where the same kind of loss is experienced though in unconnected circumstances and The Compassionate Friends for bereaved parents is one example. Some mutual help groups have the additional feature of 'activism' in pursuit of a particular social or political cause; Mothers Against Drunk Driving (MADD) in the USA, primarily grassroots and volunteer driven, is one such example. Often a sense of lack of understanding by the rest of society about the true impact of their loss draws members together and provides the impetus for their campaigns. This kind of group can become a powerful lobby for both legal and policy change.

Mutual help groups are shaped by experiential rather than professional knowledge where expertise is recognised in terms of 'having been there oneself'. This does, on one level, challenge the contention that all grief is unique but, on another, acknowledges that some types of grief experience may only be accessible in emotional terms by those 'in the same boat'. Having experienced the sudden death of my mother at the age of eight, I can remember finding myself some years later in the position of helper and supporter to a school classmate whose mother was killed in the Paris air disaster. I knew what it felt like – the terrible shock and emptiness, longing just to see her again and the complete disorientation. I suppose we formed a support group of two and, having been by that time motherless for quite a few years, I had developed coping strategies of sorts and so had 'seniority' in the support relationship that my classmate told me a long time afterwards had helped to 'get her through'.

The image of an angry but positive bereaved person in the role of activist or committed group member can challenge the over-emphasis sometimes placed on professionally skilled bereavement support. Walter (1999) argues that implicit within many bereavement mutual help groups is criticism of professional approaches that draw heavily on theoretical and regulated frameworks to guide practice. As part of the professional approach that incorporates ideas about 'training', 'effectiveness', 'accountability', 'standards' and possibly 'target setting', the real-life needs of bereaved people may become secondary, subsumed within discourses of expert knowledge tied to theoretical models that may not feel meaningful or relevant to the bereaved person. Indeed, though not part of a group system of mutual help, Walter's (1996) model of grief informed by a durable biography of the deceased whereby the bereaved talk about the dead person with those who knew them (as discussed in Chapter Five) and who may themselves also be grieving, resonates with this approach by virtue of being a 'community of feeling' (Walter, 1999, p. 189).

Despite the proliferation of mutual help groups and the widely reported benefits for those who join them, Walter (1999) offers a word of caution about the danger of over-involvement. For some the functioning of the group can become a dominant life interest with issues of dependency and a sense of 'compulsion' to maintain ongoing association with the group a potential concern. This returns us to the dual concepts of 'letting go' and 'holding on' to the dead person discussed in the previous chapter, and we are reminded that for some bereaved people, although their grief may change over time, it endures for the remainder of their life and may be a defining factor in shaping how they see both themselves and their future. Continued membership of a mutual help group may thus act as support and as validation of a changed self-identity, as might be the case with widowhood.

Bereavement services in the UK

The organisation of bereavement services within the UK is fragmented, and characterised by a mix of provision across the state, voluntary and commercial sectors with no single 'standard' operating model. Under guidance from the Department of Health contained in the document *When a Patient Dies: Advice on Developing Bereavement Services in the NHS*, NHS Trusts and Boards (in Scotland) are required to put in place systems, policies and practices to ensure high quality bereavement services. The nature and extent of this provision vary across different Trusts/Boards and regions but all hospitals are now expected to have in place a section or department to oversee this area of work. In many cases, chaplains deliver a significant part of this provision and, as discussed in Chapter Four, care of bereaved people is perceived by some chaplains to be a core part of their role. A report by the Department of Health (DOH, 2005) highlights that concerns about care surrounding the death of a patient constitute 54% of complaints about hospitals and one response has been the establishment in 2005 of the Bereavement Services Association to provide a network for all those providing bereavement support services.

As discussed above, bereavement support can take different forms and the voluntary sector has a long-established history of provision. For example, all hospices now offer dedicated bereavement support; one hospice where I have links aims to offer support through weekly group meetings throughout the first year of bereavement, in recognition that the first year, with its milestones of birthdays and anniversaries, may be particularly difficult. The Maggie's Centres, first established in Scotland to support people living with cancer, operate bereavement support groups as part of their wider programme, which is solely dependent on charitable and corporate giving. Some faith groups provide dedicated bereavement support for members of their communities and the Jewish Bereavement Counselling Service, for example, was established in response to a perceived need for a more culturally specific service for that client group.

Perhaps the best-known provider of bereavement support is the national charity Cruse, founded in 1958 by Margaret Torrie specifically as a support group for widows. In the late 1980s its remit was extended so that any bereaved person, not just widows, could access their services, described in their literature as a 'comprehensive service of counselling by trained and selected people, advice on practical matters and opportunities for social support'. Arnason (2001), at the time of his article, notes that the organisation receives over a £1million in grants from businesses and various government offices. The organisation's website (Cruse, 2009) states that it now has 23 branches in Scotland (under the auspices of Cruse Bereavement Care Scotland) and runs a training and education programme aimed at both its volunteer staff and service users. This is part of a UK-wide network of 134 local branches and over 5,500 volunteers with 80,000 enquiries/users of their service every year. Although local branches have autonomy over how they organise their affairs, standards of work and policies are overseen by the Head Office in Surrey.

Counselling that adopts the person-centred approach described above is the most important part of Cruse's work and those who counsel for Cruse do so as volunteers. They are required to complete training in the areas of grief and counselling skills as part of a selection process to assess their suitability as probation counsellors. As with all counselling practice, they are required to develop their practice through reflection, regular supervision and further training that may include specific areas of practice, such as, for example, supporting bereaved children. Work with clients is set within a framework that recommends weekly meetings lasting an hour with an initial contract for a specific number of sessions agreed between client and counsellor. Counselling usually takes place in the client's home and is governed by the ethical precept of confidentiality, a core value of the organisation. Clients are often referred by GPs or social services and this can occur at any stage following bereavement. The emphasis of this work appears to be on supporting the emotional response to bereavement and the extent to which specific grief models (such as Worden's (1982) task approach discussed in the previous chapter) inform this work is not clear from information that I have been able to access. Given that counsellors receive mandatory education and training about different social and theoretical understandings of grief, there may be an expectation that these will be utilised in different ways with individual clients. Although the training provided by Cruse to its volunteer counselling workforce is not professionally accredited, it operates on a professional basis as indicated by the lengthy and rigorous selection process.

Supporting bereaved children and young people

The final topic of this chapter is the particular support needs of children and young people. Discussion in earlier chapters has not looked specifically at the ways in which death and dying impact on children and some might argue that this topic deserves a whole separate, possibly even larger, volume of its own. In order to situate understanding of ways that children and young people can be effectively supported in bereavement, it is useful to briefly explore ideas about how children develop understanding about death before considering some of the different types of support that may be helpful.

Children and young people come into contact with death from a very young age in 'their' world of television, film, storybooks, computer games and various forms of play as well as through hearing adults talking to each other. Often early attempts at making sense of death come about through the experience of a pet dying or seeing a dead animal. Through this kind of loss, children can begin to recognise and process some of the characteristics and consequences of death, although not many children in the West will experience at first hand the death of someone close to them. Although there are no statistics available about the number of children in Scotland who are bereaved of a parent, recent figures for the UK as a whole show that 53 children are bereaved of a parent every day and 13% of children aged between 5 and 15 have experienced the death of a grandparent (ONS quoted in Pilgrim, 2006, p. 2), but this is still a small proportion.

Children of the same age differ widely in their behaviour and development and this makes it difficult to fit children's understanding and perception of death into fixed age categories. The psychologist Maria Nagy (1948) conducted one of the first and most comprehensive research studies into the views of death held by children between the ages of two and nine. Her research remains a seminal work in this area and she identifies three stages of children's developing understanding of the meaning of death.

Up until around the age of five children are curious about death but they do not understand that death is final and that the dead do not come back to life again.

By the age of eight or nine children start to develop a deeper understanding about what death means and this often includes an understanding that death is the end of life and that it is final.

From the age of nine or ten children have a fairly complete understanding that death is final and the end of bodily life. Children of this age would also be aware that death is universal – everyone dies in the end.

The experience of bereavement of older children and young people has been the subject of recent research by Ribbens McCarthy (2006). She refers to the broad category of adolescence which she broke down into early adolescence (10–14 years) and middle adolescence (15–17 years). A key feature of these years is transition, with young people experiencing bodily changes and changes in the way they engage with their families and school as they begin to move through into adulthood. This stage of a young person's life is very much focused on looking towards the future, particularly in relation to making choices about training and education. The death of someone close during these teenage years can be experienced as a threat to security and the 'taken-for-grantedness' and 'safety' of everyday life.

Although the needs of bereaved children will vary depending on the particular context of the bereavement, their age and family and cultural background, it is useful to identify different types of needs. These fall broadly into six categories: practical, physical, emotional, intellectual, social and spiritual.

Practical needs: These will vary depending on the relationship of the bereaved child to the deceased. If it is a sibling who has died, for example, issues such as sleeping alone in what was formerly a shared bedroom or travelling to and from school alone may present challenges. Where the death is that of a parent who is also the main carer a child may have to get used to a new family routine that may involve different care arrangements, such as going to a childminder after school. Other practical concerns children may have relate to being able to continue their leisure and sports interests.

Physical needs: Symptoms such as headaches, feeling sick or loss of appetite can be grief-related and require medical attention. Tiredness, caused by fear of sleeping, interrupted sleep and the experience of nightmares, can be debilitating for children. Fatigue and an associated lack of concentration may also affect children's and young people's progress at school. For some bereaved children, the use of alcohol or drugs may become an issue.

Emotional needs: These will vary in type and intensity. Children may be angry, confused, anxious, sad and insecure. The desire for a return to some kind of normality in their lives is paramount. In this emotionally disrupted and unsettled state that may last for a long time, children will need reassurance that other family members will not also die. Providing children with comfort and the opportunity to express their emotions, ask questions and be involved in decisions that affect them are central to meeting emotional needs. Where children are sent away to relatives or friends or not told about or allowed to attend the funeral, their grief may be disenfranchised (see Chapter Five).

Intellectual needs: These relate to providing children and young people with information about the circumstances of the death and how this has occurred. Part of this process should allow for children to ask questions and may involve the conveying of the information several times to embed understanding.

Social needs: The social needs of bereaved children and young people may be complex when their daily home life is disrupted and family relationships are strained or even severed. Bereaved children may not feel able to invite friends to their home and some may want to withdraw from friends, feeling that they are different from their peers. Their behaviour may also change with them becoming withdrawn, aggressive and angry. Adolescents, bereaved of a parent, may feel the need to emotionally care for the surviving parent and this can alter their social interaction with friends. When teenagers lose a friend they may feel an intense need to 'be together' to support each other and strengthen group identity as one way of affirming life (Ribbens McCarthy, 2006).

Spiritual needs: The spiritual needs of children will vary across age groups. Younger children, although not able to verbalise questions about the meaning of life, may still ask why the person has died. Where a family holds religious beliefs such concerns may be framed by questions such as 'why has he or she been taken?'. In this context picturing heaven as the place where the dead now live may be a source of spiritual comfort. Being given the opportunity to remember the dead person may also be spiritually comforting. Bereaved teenagers, with a view to their future, may review their choices as well as their relationship with the deceased.

Central to these different needs are the issues of change and transition. When children lose someone close to them their lives are irrevocably changed and learning to live with the loss becomes part of each stage of their development. Communicating openly with bereaved children is now seen as a key component of supporting them in their grief, which may be prolonged and sustained. This support is usually provided by adults and the way that adults interact with children will differ according to whether they are the child's parent, a family friend, teacher, doctor or local faith leader. Parents usually have the most regular contact with children and are closest to them, especially in the case of younger children. Because of this they are expected to have the main responsibility to help children come to terms with their loss. Where children live in a re-formed family and experience the loss of a parent or family member whom they do not live with, this support needs to be sensitive to take account of earlier separation. This may be difficult where the wider family has experienced conflict. Where the death of a brother or sister has occurred, parents themselves may be overwhelmed with grief and may not be able to offer comfort and reassurance to the remaining children. In many cases they will be feeling vulnerable and in need of practical and emotional support. Children are strongly affected by the behaviour of those around them and when they see their parents openly grieving and unable to give them attention this can make them feel insecure and anxious. In this situation parents may benefit from the support of other relatives, friends and neighbours to help them, along with a range of professional 'helpers'. Kissane and Bloch (2002) attest to the complexity of family grief, and offer an authoritative and widely researched critique of different models of family-focused grief therapy that may be of value to readers who have this as a special interest.

In recent years an increasing number of organisations and support groups have been established to provide dedicated support to bereaved children and young people. Many of these organisations are located in the voluntary sector as registered charities and some originated as self-help groups developing into different types of structured provision offering a range of practical and emotional advice. With recent technical innovations, particularly the digital revolution, that have given rise to new media forms such as organisational and personal websites, email, blogs, texting and online chatrooms, the possibilities that these open up for non face-to-face support may begin to transform both informal and professional approaches in this area. For example, the website of the UK Children's Charity ChildLine, a 24-hour help line for children in distress or danger, now has a section entitled 'When someone dies' that includes comments from children who have experienced the death of someone they love. This type of support can be accessed at any time and is an 'instant' resource.

With the growth of this type of community/voluntary sector support, we are led to ask what it does that is different from conventional support organisations. The work of the child bereavement charity Winston's Wish, for example, suggests that shared experience and the opportunity for bereaved children to meet other bereaved children are central to its effectiveness. A key feature is that individual experience becomes shared experience that then becomes shared knowledge, which may facilitate a particular type of belonging, and this is a dominant feature of mutual help groups such as those discussed above. One consequence of this is that bereaved children may find themselves helping and supporting each other (as I found many years ago). Rolls (2009) develops this theme, making the point that some bereavement services, whether provided by the statutory or voluntary sector, can offer bereaved children an opportunity to have a shared status as members of a larger community. The concept of self-help is linked to an understanding that nobody knows better than we do how we feel about ourselves or our situation. Others most likely to understand are those who have had similar experiences. The extent to which this principle can be expected to inform policy development in the broader area of death, dying and bereavement is one of the themes of Chapter 7, the last chapter of this volume.

Issues for Policy and Practice

The preceding chapters have drawn on a wide theoretical base to discuss the social and practice context of death, dying and bereavement within the UK, with particular focus on Scotland. Thus far reference has been made to some of the broad policy initiatives that frame different types of health and social care professional practice in this general area, but it is the purpose of this last chapter to examine the issue of policy as a separate topic in greater detail.

In contemporary Britain death and dying are regulated by both legislation and policy. For example, it is a legal requirement that all deaths that occur in the UK have to be certified by a medical practitioner with the cause of death stated on the death certificate. In Scotland, where there is difficulty in determining the cause of death a post-mortem (or autopsy) may be carried out. This is often done at the request of the central Procurator Fiscal as part of an enquiry to determine if further investigations are appropriate. In England and Wales relevant deaths are referred to the local coroner to ascertain cause. A coroner is a judicial officer who is responsible for investigating deaths (particularly those that happen under unusual circumstances). Post-mortems are carried out by pathologists, doctors who specialise in disease diagnosis and the identification of the cause of death. If a post-mortem is ordered by a coroner it must take place by law, whether the next of kin give their agreement or not; if, however, a post-mortem is requested by a hospital for research purposes to explore complicated disease mechanisms, written consent from the deceased's next of kin is required before this can proceed.

The Human Tissue Act (2006 for Scotland and 2004 for England and Wales) is legislation that makes consent the fundamental principle underpinning the lawful storage and use of body parts, organs and tissue from the living or the deceased for specified health-related purposes. It also covers the removal of such material from the deceased. Under the auspices of the Act the Human Tissue Authority was established in 2005 to regulate all matters pertaining to the legislation, which came into being partly as a response to malpractice uncovered in 1999 at Alder Hey Children's Hospital in Liverpool, where autopsy materials had been retained without specific authorisation. The area of tissue retention and organ donation is one that raises a whole raft of ethical issues for practice and it is not possible within this volume to consider these in depth, though other commentators (see, for example, Sque and Payne, 2007) offer a comprehensive critique.

Assisted suicide and euthanasia are two types of death that have in recent times been the subject of much legal debate and media coverage. In the UK deaths that occur in these ways are not legally sanctioned. Assisted suicide is when the person who dies administers the means of death themselves but is helped by another person, who may subsequently be prosecuted for their criminal action. Euthanasia occurs when the death is instigated by the dying person, who sees it as being in their best interests, but the means of bringing about death are administered by another person. Leming and Dickinson (2007, p. 305) offer a succinct definition of the further sub-categorisations of both *active* and *passive* euthanasia as follows: *active* euthanasia is 'a direct action that causes death in accordance with the stated or implied wishes of the terminally ill patient' whereas *passive* euthanasia is 'the withholding of treatment, which, in essence hastens death and allows the individual to die "naturally"'. The debate about euthanasia centres on its contested meanings, which range from good death to murder, with this increasingly now conceptualised by 'the right to die' critique.

Space does not allow for developed consideration of the full range of issues connected to death and dying that now fall within the UK legislative framework. However, the brief discussion above is offered to illustrate that, while death and dying is increasingly socially constructed primarily as individual experience, it is nevertheless one that is legally constituted with a requirement on the part of health professionals to verify and record its cause and other associated possible issues post-death. The remainder of this concluding chapter will focus on the importance and relevance of policy initiatives for practice, particularly related to end-of-life care, but is prefaced by a brief discussion about why policy matters and the ways in which policy directly influences the allocation of resources and the delivery of care.

Why policy?

Starting with the question of why there is a need for policy may seem unneces-sary but in a recent teaching session with undergraduate students studying a death and dying course, most of whom were practising in health and social care, I was surprised by the lack of understanding shown about why policy matters, what purpose it serves and what may be its advantages and disadvan-tages. It is not possible to explore all of these dimensions here but there is benefit in addressing some of these points to establish a conceptual base for the more detailed discussion of end-of-life policy initiatives below.

Policies can be understood to be guidance or plans of action usually as part of a document with clearly identified outcomes; these are used in a whole range of settings and activities both in the public and private sectors. Individual corporate institutions will have a range of policies covering recruitment, safety and workplace conduct of employees: these matters are similarly governed by policies within health and social care, where the main employers are those in the public sector, such as hospital trusts and, in the case of social services, local authorities. In the context of health and social care, policies are designed to support and protect both workers and service users, shaping expectations as well as responsibilities. Each policy will be a distillation of alternative possibili-ties expressed in terms of formal aims and actions required to meet those aims. Policies are not made and developed in a vacuum and almost without exception, health and social care policy builds on earlier policies that, in light of changing demographics or medical treatment options, for example, need refining to reflect the changing context in which health care is delivered. In some cases lessons learned from the implementation of earlier policies are reflected in what policy-makers see as improved policy that takes account of the shortcomings or failures of previous ideas. In this respect policy-making can be seen as responsive as well as proactive and may be the result of an inquiry, recommendations arising from research or a committee report into a particular issue. In the health sector these official inquiries usually involve wide-based consultation with members of statutory, voluntary, academic and professional groups as well as service users. At a strategic level, policy-making is also political in nature, reflecting the priorities and interests of the government executive (Althaus *et al.*, 2007).

Broadly speaking, policies involve setting operating standards that in health care terms are referred to as standards of practice. These standards are increas-ingly evidence-based, pointing to a growing emphasis on practitioners being able to answer the question 'how do we know?' in order to develop good, if not, best practice. Policies enable stronger monitoring and reviewing processes to evaluate the effectiveness of service provision with a view to exposing and minimising unsatisfactory practice as well as 'corruption' or abuses of care. In terms of the potential for abuse within care relationships, policies in this area remind us that vulnerable people are often not the active and empowered consumers of care that government policy documents sometimes assume and this may be especially the case with patients who are approaching the end of life. From the perspective of the health care worker, the demands of policies may result in forms of defensive practice that may not serve the best interests of service users or may have contradictory effects on 'good' care practice. As an example, the policy requirement of accountability has become more prominent with the advent of an increasingly litigious society. Being fully accountable for one's practice, which may include giving medication and undertaking regular patient observations, entails careful recording of personal and clinical inform-ation, sometimes excessively so. This may reduce the amount of time available for the one-to-one caring interaction between patient and health care worker that is highly valued.

End-of-life care policy in Scotland

In its recommendations, the report from NHS Scotland (2008) *Living and Dying Well: a National Action Plan for Palliative and End of Life Care in Scotland* highlights the importance of adopting a cohesive approach to planning and delivering end-of-life care across Scotland. It cites entrenched cultural resistance to acknowledging the reality of death and dying as integral parts of life as a historical obstacle to this, but notes that 70% of people in Scotland now believe that death and dying is not discussed enough (SPPC, 2003). Such views, the plan argues, indicate a gradual but increasing public awareness that, unless these issues are discussed more openly, it will be difficult to provide appropriate care and support services to both dying people and their families.

The importance of different kinds of 'practice planning' to underpin improvements in the delivery of end-of-life care is highlighted within the Scottish Action Plan. The Plan draws on a number of 'best practice' approaches outlined in the NHS End of Life Care Programme (2008) that details policy in this area for England and Wales. Findings discussed in the NHS End of Life Care Programme (2008) note that a majority of people approaching the end of their life wish to be cared for outside of hospital with many preferring their own home as the place of care (see also Chapter One). Reducing the amount of time that those who are dying spend unnecessarily in hospital could release resources available to provide effective and more comprehensive support in their own home. The report found that information on people's wishes is often not captured or shared and a lack of services to support them at home (particularly related to symptom management) may lead to unplanned and unwanted hospital admissions. In addition, there is a lack of training of frontline staff in delivering basic end-of-life care. The report comments that only 29% of doctors and 18% of nurses receive pre-registration training in end-of-life care and also that there is a lack of formal training for staff working in care homes. The report suggests that much current end-of-life care is seen as a specialist 'expert' skill but that this should change so that a broad range of health care workers, not just those working within dedicated palliative care settings, should be competent to deliver this care. It is therefore a priority to increase resources for the education and training of the general health and care workforce as a whole in practice related to end-of-life care.

This priority may challenge the occupational capacity-building that underpins the careers of palliative care professionals, giving rise to conceptual and practical tensions. Their role as death and dying educators of the health and social care workforce beyond the hospice movement is already in train, though only to a limited extent and often in relation to cancer. A related point made by Field and Addington-Hall (2000) is that there has been reluctance on the part of some specialist palliative care practitioners to extend palliative care more generally to a whole range of terminal conditions other than cancer. Dilution of expertise is cited as one justification. Furthermore, for the general health workforce the emphasis of their practice is on discourses of treatment, cure and rehabilitation and this is in contrast to the ethos of palliative care that accepts death as 'normal'.

Three practice initiatives in particular have informed policy development in both the NHS Scotland (2008) *Living and Dying Well: a National Action Plan for Palliative and End of Life Care in Scotland* and the NHS End of Life Care Programme (2008); these are outlined below.

> *The Gold Standards Framework (GSF)* is a systematic evidence-based approach to optimising the care for patients nearing the end of life in the community living in their own home or in residential care (Gold Standards Framework, 2009). The emphasis of this framework is on the optimisation of the local primary care team's support to avoid re-admission of the dying person to hospital. This framework

is applicable to patients with any advanced illness and is operated on a multi-professional basis and functions in a sequence of steps or stages. The first is to identify when patients are in the last stage of their lives and in need of supportive/palliative care. The second is to assess their needs and preferences by listening to them and proactively helping them think ahead and the third step is to help plan their care using advance care plans.

The Liverpool Care Pathway for the Dying Patient (LCP) is an integrated care pathway for the dying person that was recommended in the policy White Paper 'Our Health, Our Care, Our Say' (2006). The LCP was developed in partnership by the specialist palliative care team at the Royal Liverpool and Broadgreen University Hospitals NHS Trust and the Marie Curie Hospice, Liverpool. Following palliative care principles (see Chapter Two) it adopts a holistic approach to improving knowledge of the dying process and to improving care in the last days of life. Although the LCP was originally applied to the care of cancer patients in the acute environment, it has been adapted and disseminated across all care settings for a range of conditions. The LCP is practice-focused providing guidance on issues that include symptom control, comfort measures, anticipatory prescribing of medication, discontinuation of inappropriate interventions and care of the family.

The Preferred Place of Care Plan (PPC) has been re-named the Preferred Priorities for Care and is a document that individuals hold themselves and take with them if they receive care in different places. The document has space for patients to record their wishes, reflections and preferences about their care including what would be their preferred place to die. The aim of the plan is to try and achieve continuity of care and obviate the need for a range of health care workers to ask the same repeated questions of patients. If the patient's wishes change this can be added and the entry dated to keep the plan current. The rationale for the PPC has been included within the NHS End of Life Care Programme (2008) and has informed its central tenet of respecting the choice of individuals.

Discussion of a range of practice issues within the Scottish Action Plan draws on clinical understandings of different disease pathways or 'trajectories'.

Three main disease trajectories are identified: the relatively predictable cancer trajectory of diagnosis, treatment, possible remission and final deterioration is now well understood; the organ failure trajectory with critical events such as unscheduled hospital admissions and readmissions; the prolonged frailty/ dementia trajectory that might include significant deterioration in function and increased need for carer support, referral for specialist advice or admission to a care home. Developing understanding among health care professionals of the ways in which those living with the latter two disease trajectories can be offered palliative care is seen as a particular challenge. Recognition that patients on any of these disease trajectories are likely to move between primary, secondary and tertiary care during the course of illness is seen as an important principle for flexible and responsive co-ordination of care and is fully acknowledged within the Action Plan. Patients' relationships with these care regimes may also not be staged and sequential, with patients at any one time being cared for by primary care teams and by condition-specific specialists. In respect of primary care teams the need for enhanced skills development from core training, such as syringe driver training and verification of expected death, is recognised as central to providing appropriate care.

The Action Plan outlines twenty-four recommendations or 'Actions' designed to support a radical overhaul of end of life care. These are structured within five broad themes:

- assessment and review of palliative and end-of-life care needs;
- planning and delivery of care for patients with palliative and end-of-life care needs;
- communication and co-ordination;
- education, training and workforce development;
- implementation and future developments.

The underpinning precepts of the strategy are those of locality, responsiveness, flexibility, partnership and education. The ways in which these concepts are embedded within the strategy are considered with reference to some of the recommendations outlined below.

Action 2 – NHS Boards, through palliative care networks and Community Health Partnerships (CHPs), should ensure that patients identified with palliative and end of life care needs are appropriately assessed and reviewed in all care settings using recognised tools currently available.

An example of good practice in improving assessment is the initiative by NHS Forth Valley and the Managed Clinical Network for palliative care in developing a checklist for embarking on end-of-life treatment (CELT). This decision-making framework facilitates the transition from active treatment to end-of-life care and links the Gold Standard Framework and the Liverpool Care pathway. The CELT framework highlights the importance of excluding reversible causes of decline and can be reused in the event of further deterioration in the patient's condition. This practice innovation exemplifies the effectiveness of partnership working.

Action 6 – NHS Boards and CHPs should take steps, including the use of Patient Group Directions (PGDs) and Just in Case boxes where appropriate, to facilitate the use of anticipatory prescribing to enhance patient care and aid the prevention of unnecessary crises and unscheduled hospital admissions.

Locality, responsiveness and flexibility are features of the above recommendation. NHS Lanarkshire is in the process of introducing PGDs to allow community nurses, working out of hours, the ability to administer medicines to alleviate symptoms such as nausea, agitation and respiratory secretions commonly experienced at the end of life, in order to prevent unnecessary 'emergency' hospital admissions. A further example of assessing and planning palliative care needs is the work undertaken under the auspices of the NHS Highland Anticipatory Care Project. The project identifies an 'at risk admission' population using primary and secondary care data, called the Casefinder. The anticipatory care team helps assess the needs of patients and their families and plans for appropriate interventions to support them in accessing services to meet those needs. As a result there has been a quantified reduction in admissions, readmissions and occupied bed days for the 100 patients who have been followed through over an eight-month period.

Action 21 – NHS Education for Scotland (NES) will work in partnership with NHS Boards, Palliative care Networks, Practice Development Units and Quality Improvement Teams to support the managed implementation and expansion of the LCP or equivalent integrated care pathway across all care settings.

An example of an education and partnership project based on the aims of the above recommendation is the Care Homes project of NHS Forth Valley that has an active local Managed Clinical Network (MCN) for palliative care. This brings together representatives from all care settings as well as other stakeholders including representation from the private care home sector to consider best practice in this area. Examples of this work include implementation of the Liverpool Care Pathway in 40% of homes, inclusion of care homes in the roll out of the Mckinley Syringe pump, and development of bespoke education packages for care homes.

The Action Plan prioritises the activity of assessment as pivotal in identifying those who are likely to benefit from palliative and end-of-life care. It recommends that incorporating the element of assessment as part of regular clinical management, with a view to 'diagnosing dying', is important in ensuring that a person's needs are fully met in the end phase of life with the provision of planned care rather than care provided as response to critical events or sudden significant deterioration (NHS Scotland, 2008, p. 9). This approach, the plan notes, will be underpinned by a greater readiness on the part of the health care team to acknowledge that the patient is entering the dying phase. Without this greater awareness, the delivery of skilled high quality care in all settings will be difficult to implement. As Ellershaw and Ward (2003) note, diagnosing dying is seldom easy but the expertise in this area developed within hospices make hospice-based care teams well placed to have a central role in planning and implementing appropriate care for the dying phase.

As discussed in Chapter Two, when someone is facing death the importance of communication between the patient, their family and health care professionals is seen as critically important in the decision-making process. Where patients may move between primary and secondary or tertiary care teams, the value of identifying a named health or social care professional to plan and co-ordinate care has been acknowledged within the Action Plan and this is currently being implemented for all patients identified as having end-of-life care needs. The issue of transition from one care setting to another is recognised within the Action Plan as being potentially problematic in terms of ensuring that patients' records (including the preferences about care and treatment options and patient and carer consent) are kept up to date and are fully accessible to clinicians. The Scottish Government is currently facilitating the development of an electronic Palliative Care Summary (ePCS) and this is being piloted in NHS Grampian. Subject to positive evaluation, the intention is for this to be rolled out across Scotland by the end of 2009.

In recognition of the challenges presented by dispersed populations, the Action Plan draws heavily on the principles that underpin the Gold Standards Framework (GSF) with its strategies, tasks and enabling tools designed to help primary care teams improve the organisation and quality of care for patients in the last stages of life in the community. It identifies general practices as the key unit from which effective end-of-life care policy can be implemented. This local work will be supported by Community Health Partnerships (CHP), which have been established by NHS Boards to be instrumental in the redesign of services. In particular, CHPs are intended to offer integration of primary care and specialist services as well as social care. CHPs will be instrumental in supporting general practices to use upgraded IT systems to record patients' palliative care needs, plan review dates and assist multi-disciplinary teams. The emphasis on a community model of care is also directed towards supporting the needs of informal carers, whose needs are largely unmet and may exceed those of the dying person (Cavaye, 2006; Koffman *et al.*, 2008).

Alongside the emphasis on the GSF the 2008 plan supports the use of the Liverpool Care Pathway (LCP) as good practice in all care settings and has committed resources for the education and training of the health workforce to embed knowledge of its principles. The report by the Scottish Partnership for Palliative Care submitted to the Scottish Executive in May 2007, as a major contribution to the 2008 report, has as a central theme generalists and specialists working together to ensure that high quality palliative care is available to all and that specialist provision is available to patients with complex needs. It adopts the principles of equity and justice giving people with life-limiting conditions other than cancer equal priority for receiving palliative care.

Following the release of the 2008 Action Plan there have been some significant developments in implementing its provision. In recognition of the need for strong leadership the appointment until June 2010 of a National Clinical lead for Palliative and End of Life Care has been made. Also for each of the fourteen NHS Boards an Executive Lead for Palliative and End of Life Care has been identified. Additionally, short-life collaborative working groups have been set up to monitor implementation of different areas of the Action Plan with a requirement to report their findings by March 2010.

In summary, end-of-life care policy in England and Wales is adopting similar principles to those that inform policy in Scotland with an increased emphasis on 'local', patient preferences for place of care and the need for working across traditional occupational and professional boundaries. Central to this goal is an increase in resources for training and education across the health workforce to enhance skill levels of generalists. The policy imperative that access to care should be based on patients' needs rather than on disease diagnosis highlights the importance both of needs assessment and of a needs-based palliative care strategy to embrace multidisciplinarity and cross-professional working. The 2008 Action Plan makes clear that management of care will be led by community nurses who may be supported by specialists and who will be trained to use new technology in providing palliative care to patients in remote communities. This may include the use of telemedicine whereby medical information is transferred via telephone, the internet or other networks for the purpose of consulting or guiding clinical procedures. Other potential applications are remote observation of the patient and the acquiring of medical data (such as medical images) for transmission to a doctor for offline assessment. Recognition within the Action Plan of the potential benefits of a range of electronic working signals the importance of Scotland's geography in planning and delivering care.

Some concluding thoughts

An underpinning precept of the above policies is the respect for patient autonomy, one of Beauchamp and Childress's (2001) four ethical principles for health care practice discussed in Chapter Two. Respecting patient choice against a background of scarce resources, such as is the case within the NHS, may be a significant challenge for practice, both at an individual practitioner level and at a strategic level. Issues connected to levels of staffing and education and training inform the ongoing debate about practice, specifically about improvements in practice. Returning to the topic of spirituality discussed in Chapter Four, the temporal dimension is of particular importance for people who are dying. Health care workers being able to spend time to 'just be' with dying patients is understood to be important, yet so much end-of-life care is associated with symptom management. Clinical instruments such as the oxygen mask, the catheter and the syringe driver materially operate to diminish the relational encounter between the medic/carer and the dying person (Edgley, 2003, p. 451). Of further note is that no amount of policy that essentially addresses 'what' and 'how to' issues can imbue individual health care workers with empathy, kindness and sensitivity and, as many patients comment (see Randall and Downie, 2006), it is these personal attributes that can so often make the difference to those who are dying and who may be experiencing significant suffering. This was discussed in Chapter Four in relation to spiritual care and has relevance more generally to all aspects of end-of-life care.

The preceding discussion of policy ideas and initiatives highlights the increased profile death and dying now has within the wider health policy arena and shows how the concepts of health and well-being are gradually informing understanding of what it may mean to 'die well'. This does mark a significant break from earlier times where the needs of dying people have not been wholly or separately recognised but subsumed and 'fitted in' alongside the pressing concerns of medicine in its attempts at cure and the prolonging of life. The role of the hospice movement (discussed in Chapter Three) has been pivotal in influencing the way in which complex systems of health and social care support the experience of death and dying. In particular, the concept of total pain (discussed in Chapter Two) which acknowledges that dying may be complex, 'messy' and difficult, not just for the dying person but for their family too, has had a profound impact on policy that now recognises that a range of practical and social issues, as well as health concerns, contribute to a nexus of need.

A fundamental feature of total pain is the experience of suffering and it is this aspect of dying that care practitioners find difficult because it is so personal and uniquely differentiated. As Wilkinson (2005, p. 16) notes, 'while being able to recognise and respond to the outward signs of a person's distress, we can never actually enter into the realms of their personal experience of suffering'. In this sense suffering that is characterised by pain is not 'shareable', being 'unspeakable' (Frank, 2001, p. 354), carrying with it the potential to strike at the heart of our humanity by disrupting every aspect of personhood (Cassell, 1982). In the final analysis there may be no policy or technique adequate to the task of eliminating or even minimising suffering and perhaps we are in danger of expecting too much of health workers if the resolution of suffering should come to form part of their remit. Also, given the cultural mix of contemporary UK society, such a focus may for some dying people be less than appropriate. This leaves us with the question of what then is at the core of the role of health and social care professionals in their work with people who are dying or bereaved. Through my own personal experience and years of researching and reading about this topic I have come to see that it is accompaniment that is the essence of this work. By that I mean being alongside, offering one's whole self to listen and just 'be' with the other person at what is an extraordinary and, in the case of those facing death, usually short time in their life.

References

Addington-Hall, J. (2004) 'Referral patterns and access to specialist palliative care', in S. Payne, J. Seymour and C. Ingleton (eds) (2004) *Palliative Care Nursing: Principles and Evidence for Practice*, Maidenhead: Open University Press, pp. 90-107

Althaus, C., Bridgman, P. and Davis, G. (2007) *The Australian Policy Handbook*, 4th edition, Crows Nest, New South Wales: Allen & Unwin

Altschuler, J. (2005) 'Illness and loss within the family', in P. Firth, G. Luff and D. Oliviere (eds) (2005) *Loss, Change and Bereavement in Palliative Care*, Maidenhead: Open University Press, pp. 53-65

Andersson, B. and Ohlen, J. (2005) 'Being a hospice volunteer', *Palliative Medicine*, Vol. 19, No. 8, pp. 602-9

Aries, P. (1981) *The Hour of our Death*, London: Allen Lane

Armstrong-Coster, A. (2004) *Living and Dying with Cancer*, Cambridge: Cambridge University Press

Arnason, A. (2001) 'The skills we need: bereavement counselling and governmentality in England', in J. Hockey, J. Katz and N. Small (eds) (2001) *Grief, Mourning and Death Ritual*, Buckingham: Open University Press, pp. 125-34

Ball, S., Bignold, S. and Cribb, A. (1996) 'Death and the Disease: inside the culture of childhood cancer', in G. Howarth and P. C. Jupp (eds) (1996) *Contemporary Issues in the Sociology of Death, Dying and Disposal*, Basingstoke: Macmillan Press Ltd

Barker, L. and Hawkett, S. (2004) 'Policy, audit, evaluation and clinical governance', in S. Payne, J. Seymour and C. Ingleton (eds) (2004) *Palliative Care Nursing*, Maidenhead: Open University Press, pp. 713-33

Bass, D. M. and Bowman, K. (1990) 'The transition from caregiving to bereavement: the relationship of care-related strain and adjustment to death', *The Gerontologist*, Vol. 30, No. 1, pp. 35-42

Beauchamp, T. and Childress, J. (2001) *Principles of Biomedical Ethics*, 5th edition, Oxford: Oxford University Press

Birtwistle, J. (2004) 'The perspective of community nurses', in S. Payne, J. Seymour and C. Ingleton (eds) (2004) *Palliative Care Nursing*, Maidenhead: Open University Press, pp. 502-20

Blanche, M. and Endersby, C. (2004) 'Refugees', in D. Oliviere and B. Monroe (eds) (2004) *Death, Dying and Social Differences*, Oxford: Oxford University Press

Bolger, M (2004) 'Offenders', in D. Oliviere and B. Monroe (eds) (2004) *Death, Dying and Social Differences*, Oxford: Oxford University Press

Bowlby, J. (1991) *Loss: Sadness and Depression* (Vol. 3 of *Attachment and Loss*), London: Penguin

Bradbury, M. (1996) 'Representations of "good" and "bad" death among death workers and the bereaved', in G. Howarth and P. C. Jupp (eds) (1996) *Contemporary Issues in the Sociology of Death, Dying and Disposal*, Basingstoke: Macmillan Press Ltd

Bradbury, M. (2000) 'The good death', in D. Dickenson, M. Johnson and J. S. Katz (eds) (2000) *Death, Dying and Bereavement*, London: Sage Publications

Bradshaw, A. (1996) 'The spiritual dimension of hospice: the secularization of an ideal', *Social Science and Medicine*, Vol. 43, No. 3, pp. 409–19

Bryant-Jefferies, R. (2006) *Counselling for Death and Dying*, Oxford: Radcliffe Publishing

Buckman, R. (2000) 'Communication in palliative care: a practical guide', in D. Dickenson, M. Johnson and J. S. Katz (eds) (2000) *Death, Dying and Bereavement*, London: Sage Publications, pp. 146–73

Bury, M. (1982) 'Chronic illness as biographical disruption', *Sociology of Health and Illness*, Vol. 4, No. 2, pp. 167–82

Buttery, T. J. and Robertson, P. S. (2005) 'Spirituality: the physiological-biological foundation', *New Directions for Teaching and Learning*, Vol. 104, pp. 37–42

Campo, J. E. (2006) 'Muslim ways of death: between the prescribed and the performed', in K. Garces-Foley (ed.) (2006) *Death and Religion in a Changing World*, Armonk, New York: M. E. Sharpe, pp. 147–77

Cassell, E. J. (1982) 'The nature of suffering and the goals of medicine', *New England Journal of Medicine*, Vol. 306, No. 11, pp. 639–45

Cassell, E. J. (1991) *The Nature of Suffering and the Goals of Medicine,* New York: Oxford University Press

Cavaye, J. (2006) *Hidden Carers*, Edinburgh: Dunedin Academic Press

CHAS (2005) Children's Hospice Association Scotland, www.chas.org.uk

Clark, D. (1993) 'Whither the hospices?', in D. Clark (ed.) (1993) *The Future for Palliative Care: Issues of Policy and Practice*, Buckingham: Open University Press, pp. 167–77

Clark, D. (1999) 'Cradled to the grave? Terminal care in the United Kingdom, 1948–67', *Mortality*, Vol. 4, No. 3, pp. 225–47

Clark, D. and Seymour, J. (1999) *Reflections on Palliative Care*, Buckingham: Open University Press

Clarkson, P. (2002) *The Transpersonal Relationship in Psychotherapy,* London: Whurr Publishers Ltd

Cobb, M. (2001) *The Dying Soul*, Buckingham: Open University Press

Cobb, M. (2004) 'The care and support of bereaved people', in S. Payne, J. Seymour and C. Ingleton (eds) (2004) *Palliative Care Nursing Principles and Evidence for Practice*, Maidenhead: Open University Press, pp. 490–520

Cobb, M. (2008) 'Spiritual Care' in M. Lloyd-Williams (ed.) (2008) *Psychosocial Issues in Palliative Care*, 2nd edition, Oxford: Oxford University Press, pp. 191–206

Cobb, M. and Legood, G. (2008) 'Spiritual and artistic care', in G. Bolton (ed.) (2008) *Dying, Bereavement and the Healing Arts*, London and Philadelphia: Jessica Kingsley, pp. 176–85

Cruse (2009) www.crusebereavementcare.org.uk (accessed 16 January 2009)

Currer, C. (2001) 'Is grief an illness? Issues of theory in relation to cultural diversity and the grieving process', in J. Hockey, J. Katz and N. Small (eds) (2001) *Grief, Mourning and Death Ritual*, Buckingham: Open University Press, pp. 49–60

Dein, S. and Abbas, S. Q. (2005) 'The stresses of volunteering in a hospice: a qualitative study', *Palliative Medicine*, Vol. 19, No.1, pp. 58–64

DeSpelder, L. A. and Strickland, A. L. (2005) *The Last Dance*, 7th edition, Boston: McGraw Hill

DOH (2005) Department of Health, *When a Patient Dies – Advice on Developing*

Bereavement Services in the NHS

Doka, K. J. (ed.) (1989) *Disenfranchised Grief: Recognizing Hidden Sorrow*, Lexington, MA: Lexington Books

Doka, K. J. (2002) *Disenfranchised Grief: New Directions, Challenges and Strategies for Practice*, Illinois: Research Press

Dosser, I. and Nicol, J. S. (2006) 'What does palliative day care mean to you?', *European Journal of Palliative Care*, Vol. 13, No. 4, pp. 152–5

Douglas, H. R., Normand, C. E., Higginson, I. J., Goodwin, D. M. and Myers, K. (2003) 'Palliative day care: what does it cost to run a centre and does attendance affect use of other services?', *Palliative Medicine*, Vol. 17, No. 7, pp. 628–37

Dyson, J., Cobb, M. and Forman, D. (1997) 'The meaning of spirituality: a literature review', *Journal of Advanced Nursing*, Vol. 26, pp. 1183–8

Edgley, C. (2003) 'Dying as deviance: an update on the relationship between terminal patients and medicine', in C. D. Bryant (ed.) (2003) *Handbook of Death and Dying*, London: Sage Publications

Ellershaw, J. E. and Garrard, E. (2004) 'Ethical issues in palliative care', *Medicine*, Vol. 32, No. 4, pp. 27–8

Ellershaw, J. E. and Ward, C. (2003) 'Care of the dying patient: the last hours or days of life', *British Medical Journal*, Vol. 326, pp. 30–4

Elliot, A. (2002) 'Putting spiritual care at the centre of the NHS', *Scottish Journal of Healthcare Chaplaincy*, Vol. 5, No. 1, pp. 15–19

Elmore, M. (2006) 'Contemporary Hindu approaches to death: living with the dead', in K. Garces-Foley (ed.) (2006) *Death and Religion in a Changing World*, Armonk, New York: M. E. Sharpe, pp. 23–44

Field, D. and Addington-Hall, J. (2000) 'Extending specialist palliative care to all?', in D. Dickenson, M. Johnson and J. S. Katz (eds) (2000) *Death, Dying and Bereavement*, London: Sage Publications Ltd, pp. 91–106

Field, D. and Copp, G. (1999) 'Communication and awareness about dying in the 1990s', *Palliative Medicine*, Vol. 13, pp. 459–68

Firth, S. (2000) 'Approaches to death in Hindu and Sikh communities in Britain', in D. Dickenson, M. Johnson and J. S. Katz (eds.) (2000) *Death, Dying and Bereavement*, London: Sage Publications, pp. 28–34

Firth, S. (2001) 'Hindu death and mourning rituals: the impact of geographic mobility', in J. Hockey, J. Katz and N. Small (eds) (2001) *Grief, Mourning and Death Ritual*, Buckingham: Open University Press, pp. 237–46

Firth, S. (2004) 'Minority ethnic communities and religious groups', in D. Oliviere and B. Monroe (eds) (2004) *Death, Dying and Social Differences*, Oxford: Oxford University Press

Frank, A.W. (1995) *The Wounded Storyteller*, Chicago, IL: University of Chicago Press

Frank, A. W. (2001) 'Can we research suffering?', *Qualitative Health Research*, Vol. 11, No. 3, pp. 353–62

Frank, A. W. (2004) *The Renewal of Generosity – Illness, Medicine and How to Live*, Chicago, IL: University of Chicago Press

Freud, S. (1984) On Metapsychology: the Theory of Psychoanalysis: 'Beyond the Pleasure Principle', 'The Ego and the Id' and Other Works, Harmondsworth: Penguin

Giddens, A. (1991) *Modernity and Self-Identity*, Cambridge: Polity Press

Glaser, B. and Strauss, S. (1965) *Awareness of Dying*, Chicago: Aldine Publishing Company

Golbert, R. (2006) 'Judaism and death: finding meaning in ritual', in K. Garces-Foley (ed.) (2006) *Death and Religion in a Changing World*, Armonk, New York: M. E. Sharpe, pp. 45–68

Gold Standards Framework (GSF), www.goldstandardsframework.nhs.uk (accessed 19 January 2009)

Goss, R. E. and Klass, D. (2006) 'Buddhisms and death', in K. Garces-Foley (ed.) (2006) *Death and Religion in a Changing World*, Armonk, New York: M. E. Sharpe, pp. 69–92

Grinyer, A. (2002) *Cancer in Young Adults: Through Parents' Eyes*, Buckingham: Open University Press

Gunaratnam, Y. (1997) 'Culture is not enough: a critique of multi-culturalism in palliative care', in D. Field, J. Hockey and N. Small (eds) (1997) *Death, Gender and Ethnicity*, London: Routledge, pp. 166–86

Gunaratnam, Y. (2008) 'From competence to vulnerability: care, ethics and elders from racialised minorities', *Mortality*, Vol. 13, No. 1, pp. 24–41

Harman, W. V. (1981) 'Death of my baby', *British Medical Journal*, Vol. 282, pp. 35–7

Hay, D. (2002) 'The spirituality of adults in Britain – recent research', *Scottish Journal of Healthcare Chaplaincy*, Vol. 5, No. 1, pp. 4–9

Hearn, J. (2001) 'Audit in palliative day care: what, why, when, how, where and who', in J. Hearn and K. Myers (eds) (2001) *Palliative Day Care in Practice*, Oxford: Oxford University Press, pp. 94–115

Heelas, P., Woodhead, L., Seel, B., Szerszynski, B. and Tusting, K. (2005) *The Spiritual Revolution: Why Religion is Giving Way to Spirituality*, Oxford: Blackwell Publishing

Higginson, I. J. (1998) 'Clinical and organizational audit in palliative care', in D. Doyle, G. Hanks and N. MacDonald (eds) (1998) *Oxford Textbook of Palliative Medicine*, 2nd edition, Oxford: Oxford University Press, pp. 67–82

Higginson, I. J. and Goodwin, D. M. (2001) 'Needs assessment in day care', in J. Hearn and K. Myers (eds) (2001) *Palliative Day Care in Practice*, Oxford: Oxford University Press, pp.12–22

Higginson, I. J., Finlay, I., Goodwin, D. M., Cook, A. M., Hood, K., Edwards, A. G., Douglas, H. R. and Norman, C. E. (2002) 'Do hospital-based palliative teams improve care for patients or families at the end of life?', *Journal of Pain and Symptom Management*, Vol. 23, No. 2, pp. 96–106

Higginson, I. J., Hearn, J., Myers, K. and Naysmith, A. (2000) 'Palliative day care: what do services do?', *Palliative Medicine*, Vol. 14, No. 4, pp. 277–86

Hockey, J. (1990) *Experiences of Death: an Anthropological Account*, Edinburgh: Edinburgh University Press

Hockey, J. (2002) 'Dying the way we live', in B. Rumbold (ed.) (2002) *Spirituality and Palliative Care*, Melbourne: Oxford University Press, pp. 51–63

Hodgson, N. A., Segal, S., Weidinger, M. and Linde, M. B. (2009) 'The social worker and chaplain during and after death', in S. Earle, C. Bartholomew and C. Komaromy (eds) (2009) *Making Sense of Death, Dying and Bereavement: an Anthology*, pp. 106–8

Holloway, M. (2007) *Negotiating Death in Contemporary Health and Social Care*, Bristol: The Policy Press

Holstein, J. and Gubrium, J. (2000) *The Self We Live By: Narrative Identity in a Postmodern World*, New York: Oxford University Press

Housing 21, www.housing21.co.uk (accessed 16 April 2009)

Howarth, G. (2007) *Death and Dying: a Sociological Introduction*, Cambridge: Polity Press

James, N. and Field, D. (1992) 'The routinization of hospice: bureaucracy and charisma', *Social Science and Medicine*, Vol. 34, No. 12, pp. 1363–75

Jarrett, N. and Payne, S. (2000) 'Creating and maintaining "optimism" in cancer care communication', *International Journal of Nursing Studies*, Vol. 37, pp. 81–90

Jeffrey, D. (2005) 'Curing and caring', in P. Webb (ed.) (2005) *Ethical Issues in Palliative Care*, 2nd edition, Abingdon: Radcliffe Publishing Ltd

Jupp, P. C. and Walter, T. (1999) 'The healthy society: 1918–1998', in P. C. Jupp and C. Gittings (eds) (1999) *Death in England*, Manchester: Manchester University Press

Katz, J. (2001) 'Nursing homes', in G. Howarth and O. Leaman (eds) (2001) *The Encyclopedia of Death and Dying*, London: Routledge

Kaufman, S. R. (2005) *And a Time to Die: How American Hospitals Shape the End of Life*, Chicago: The University of Chicago Press

Kellehear, A. (1984) 'Are we a "death-denying" society? A sociological review', *Social Science and Medicine*, Vol. 18, No. 9, pp. 713–23

Kellehear, A. (2000) 'Spirituality and palliative care: a model of needs', *Palliative Medicine*, Vol. 14, pp. 149–55

Kellehear, A. (2005) *Compassionate Cities: Public Health and End-of-Life Care*, London: Routledge

Kellehear, A. (2007) *A Social History of Dying*, Cambridge: Cambridge University Press

Kellehear, A. (2008) 'Health promotion and palliative care', in G. Mitchell (ed.) (2008) *Palliative Care: a Patient-Centered Approach*, Oxford: Radcliffe Publishing, pp. 139–56

Kennett, C. E. (2000) 'Participation in a creative arts project can foster hope in a hospice day centre', *Palliative Medicine*, Vol.14, No. 5, pp. 419–25

Kinlaw, K. (2005) 'Ethical issues in palliative care', *Seminars in Oncology Nursing*, Vol. 21, No. 1, pp. 63–8

Kissane, D. W. and Bloch, S. (2002) *Family Focused Grief Therapy*, Maidenhead: Open University Press

Kite, S., Jones, K. and Tookman, A. (1999) 'Specialist palliative care and patients with non-cancer diagnosis: the experience of a service', *Palliative Medicine*, Vol. 13, pp. 477–84

Klass, D., Silverman, P. R. and Nickman, S. L. (eds) (1996) *Continuing Bonds: New Understandings of Grief*, London: Taylor & Francis

Koffman, J., Harding, R. and Higginson, I. (2008) 'Palliative care: the magnitude of the problem', in G. Mitchell (ed.) (2008) *Palliative Care: a Patient-Centered Approach*, Oxford: Radcliffe Publishing, pp. 7–34

Kubler-Ross, E. (1970) *On Death and Dying*, London: Tavistock

Lamers, W. M. (2002) 'Defining hospice and palliative care: some further thoughts', *Journal of Pain & Palliative Care Pharmacotherapy*, Vol. 16, No. 3, pp. 65–71

Larkin, P. J. (2008) 'Family-centred care: psychosocial care for the marginalized', in M. Lloyd-Williams (ed.) (2008) *Psychosocial Issues in Palliative Care*, 2nd edition, Oxford: Oxford University Press, pp. 69–94

Larson-Miller, L. (2006) 'Roman Catholic, Anglican, and Eastern Orthodox approaches to death', in K. Garces-Foley (ed.) (2006) *Death and Religion in a Changing World*, Armonk, New York: M. E. Sharpe, pp. 93–121 ton, J. (2001) *Spirituality and Mental Health: Rediscovering a 'Forgotten' Dimension*, ondon: Jessica Kingsley Publishers

i, R. A. (2002) 'Towards clarification of the meaning of spirituality', *Journal of vanced Nursing*, Vol. 39, No. 5, pp. 500–9

npson, N. (1997) 'Masculinity and loss', in D. Field, J. Hockey and N. Small (eds) 997) *Death, Gender and Ethnicity*, London: Routledge, pp. 76–88

npson, S. (2007) 'Spirituality and Old Age', *Illness, Crisis and Loss*, Vol. 15. No. 2, . 167–78

ne, B. (2005) *The Mystical Power of Person-centred Therapy: Hope beyond Despair*, ndon: Whurr Publishers Ltd

man, A. J. and Scharpen-von Heussen, K. S. (2001) 'The role of the doctor in day re', in J. Hearn and K. Myers (eds) (2001) *Palliative Day Care in Practice*, Oxford: ford University Press, pp. 79–93

ross, R. (2003) *Introducing Palliative Care*, 4th edition, Abingdon: Radcliffe Medical ss

, B. (2008) '"Going down" and "getting deeper": physical and metaphorical location movement in relation to death and spiritual care in a Scottish hospice', *Mortality*, l. 13, No. 1, pp. 42–64

Hornstein, W. F. and Gruber, H. (2006) 'Art therapy and symptom control: a team roach', *European Journal of Palliative Care*, Vol. 13, No. 3, pp. 124–6

r, T. (1992) 'Modern death: taboo or not taboo?', *Sociology*, Vol. 25, No. 2, pp. –310

r, T. (1994) *The Revival of Death*, London: Routledge

r, T. (1996) 'A new model of grief: bereavement and biography', *Mortality*, Vol. 1, . 1, pp. 7–25

r, T. (1997) 'The ideology and organization of spiritual care: three approaches', liative Medicine, Vol. 11, pp. 21–30

r, T. (1999) *On Bereavement: the Culture of Grief*, Maidenhead: Open University ss

r, T. (2002) 'Spirituality in palliative care: opportunity or burden?', *Palliative dicine*, Vol. 16, No. 2, pp. 133–40

r, T. (2006) 'Disaster, modernity, and the media', in K. Garces-Foley (ed.) (2006) th and Religion in a Changing World, Armonk, New York: M. E. Sharpe, pp. –82

J. H. (2008) 'Journeying with Morrie: challenging notions of professional delivery piritual care at the end of life', *Illness, Crisis and Loss*, Vol. 16, No. 4, pp. 305–19

J. H. (2009a) 'Being orphaned in early adulthood', in S. Earle, C. Bartholomew C. Komaromy (eds) (2009) *Making Sense of Death, Dying and Bereavement: an hology*, London: Sage Publications, pp. 123–4

J. H. (2009b) '"I come because I can". Stories of hope from the cancer drop-in', ss, Crisis and Loss, Vol. 17, No. 2, pp. 151–68

J. H. (2009c) 'Illness and the creative arts: a critical exploration', in S. Earle, C. tholomew and C. Komaromy (eds) (2009) *Death and Dying: a Reader*, London: e Publications, pp. 102–8

J. H. (2009d) 'Meanings of spirituality at the cancer drop-in', *International Journal ualitative Studies on Health and Well-being*, Vol. 4, No. 2, pp. 86–93

tein, J. (2008) *Working with Loss, Death and Bereavement*, London: Sage lications

Lawton, J. (2000) *The Dying Process: Patients' Experiences of Palliative Care*, London: Routledge

Leming, M. R. and Dickinson, G. E. (2007) *Understanding Dying, Death and Bereavement*, 6th edition, Belmont, CA: Thomson Higher Education

Lindemann, E. (1944) 'The symptomatology and management of acute grief', *American Journal of Psychiatry*, Vol. 101, pp. 141–8

Lofland, L. (1978) *The Craft of Dying: the Modern Face of Death*, Beverly Hills: Sage Publications

Low, J., Perry, R. and Wilkinson, S. (2005) 'A qualitative evaluation of the impact of palliative care day services: the experiences of patients, informal carers, day unit managers and volunteer staff', *Palliative Medicine*, Vol. 19, No. 1, pp. 65–70

Lucke, G., Gilbert, R. B. and Barrett, R. K. (2006) 'Protestant approaches to death: overcoming death's sting', in K. Garces-Foley (ed.) (2006) *Death and Religion in a Changing World*, Armonk, New York: M. E. Sharpe, pp. 122–46

MacLeod, R. (2008) 'Setting the context: what do we mean by psychosocial care in palliative care?', in M. Lloyd-Williams (ed.) (2008) *Psychosocial Issues in Palliative Care*, Oxford: Oxford University Press, pp. 1–20

Marie Curie (2004) http://campaign.mariecurie.org.uk

Marris, P. (1974) *Loss and Change*, London: Routledge Kegan Paul

Maslow, A. (1970) *Motivation and Personality*, New York: Harper & Row

Mason, T. and Whitehead, E. (2003) *Thinking Nursing*, Maidenhead: Open University Press

Mayne, M. (2006) *The Enduring Melody*, London: Darton, Longman and Todd

McGregor, S. (2002) 'Revised guidelines on chaplaincy and spiritual care in the NHS: synopsis of the report of the working party', *Scottish Journal of Healthcare Chaplaincy*, Vol. 5, No. 1, pp. 20–3

McIntosh, J. (1977) Communication and Awareness in a Cancer Ward, New York: Prodist

McMurray, A. (2004) 'Older people', in D. Oliviere and B. Monroe (eds) (2004) *Death, Dying and Social Differences*, Oxford: Oxford University Press, pp. 63–78

McSherry, W. (2000) *Making Sense of Spirituality in Nursing Practice*, London: Churchill Livingstone

McSherry, W. (2006) 'The principal components model: a model for advancing spirituality and spiritual care within nursing and health care practice', *Journal of Clinical Nursing*, Vol. 15, pp. 905–17

McSherry, W. and Cash, K. (2004) 'The language of spirituality: an emerging taxonomy', *International Journal of Nursing Studies*, Vol. 41, No. 2, pp. 151–61

Mitchell, G., Murray, J. and Hynson, J. (2008) 'Understanding the whole person: life-limiting illness across the life cycle', in G. Mitchell (ed.) (2008) *Palliative Care: a Patient-Centered Approach*, Oxford: Radcliffe Publishing, pp. 79–108

Molyneux, D. (2007) 'And how is life going for you? – an account of subjective welfare in medicine', *Journal of Medical Ethics*, Vol. 33, pp. 568–82

Moore, J. and Purton, C. (eds) (2006) *Spirituality and Counselling: Experiential and Theoretical Perspectives*, Ross-on-Wye: PCCS Books

Mor, V., McHorney, C. and Sherwood, S. (1986) 'Secondary morbidity among the recently bereaved', *American Journal of Psychiatry*, Vol. 143, No. 2, pp. 158–63

Murray, S. A. and Sheikh, A. (2008) 'Making a difference: palliative care beyond cancer care for all at the end of life', *British Medical Journal*, Vol. 336, pp. 958–9

Myers, K. (2001) 'Future perspectives for day care', in J. Hearn and K. Myers (eds) (2001) *Palliative Day Care in Practice*, Oxford: Oxford University Press, pp. 136–52

Myers, K. and Hearn, J. (2001) 'An introduction to palliative day care: past and present', in J.Hearn and K. Myers (eds) (2001) *Palliative Day Care in Practice*, Oxford: Oxford University Press, pp. 1–11

Myrvold, K. (2006) 'Sikhism and death', in K. Garces-Foley (ed.) (2006) *Death and Religion in a Changing World*, Armonk, New York: M. E. Sharpe, pp. 178–204

Nagy, M. (1948) 'The child's theories concerning death', *Journal of Genetic Psychology*, Vol. 73, pp. 3–27

NHS End of Life Care Programme (2008), www.endoflifecareforadults.nhs.uk

NHS Scotland (2008) *Living and Dying Well: a National Action Plan for Palliative and End of Life Care in Scotland*, NHS Scotland, Edinburgh: The Scottish Government

NSO (2006) National Statistics Online, www.statistics.gov.uk

O'Connor, M. (2004) 'Transitions in status from wellness to illness, illness to wellness', in S. Payne, J. Seymour and C. Ingleton (eds) (2004) *Palliative Care Nursing Principles and Evidence for Practice*, Maidenhead: Open University Press, pp. 126–41

O'Keefe, K. (2001) 'Establishing day care', in J. Hearn and K. Myers (eds) (2001) *Palliative Day Care in Practice*, Oxford: Oxford University Press, pp. 43–58

Pargament, K. I., Murray-Swank, N. A. and Tarakeshwar, N. (2005) 'An empirically-based rationale for a spirituality-integrated psychotherapy', *Mental Health, Religion and Culture*, Vol. 8, No. 3, pp. 155–65

Parkes, C. M. (1988) 'Bereavement as a psychosocial transition: processes of adaptation to change', *Journal of Social Issues*, Vol. 44, No. 3, pp. 53–65

Parkes, C. M. (2000) 'Bereavement as a psychosocial transition: processes of adaptation to change', in D. Dickenson, M. Johnson and J. S. Katz (eds.) (2000) *Death, Dying and Bereavement*, London: Sage Publications, pp. 325–31

Payne, S. and Seymour, J. (2004) 'Overview', in S. Payne, J. Seymour and C. Ingleton (eds) (2004) *Palliative Care Nursing*, Maidenhead: Open University Press, pp. 15–38

Peberdy, A. (2000) 'Spiritual care of dying people', in D. Dickenson, M. Johnson and J. S. Katz (eds) (2000) *Death, Dying and Bereavement*, London: Sage Publications, pp. 73–81

Pilgrim, D. (2006) *Real Life Issues: Bereavement*, Richmond, Surrey: Trotman and Company Ltd

Prior, L. (2000) 'The social distribution of sentiments', in D. Dickenson, M. Johnson and J. S. Katz (eds) (2000) *Death, Dying and Bereavement*, London: Sage Publications, pp. 332–7

Randall, F. and Downie, R. S. (2000) 'The main tradition', in D. Dickenson, M. Johnson and J. S. Katz (eds) *Death, Dying and Bereavement*, London: Sage Publications, pp. 263–9

Randall, F. and Downie, R. S. (2006) *The Philosophy of Palliative Care: Critique and Reconstruction*, Oxford: Oxford University Press

Rando, A. T. (1986) *Parental Loss of a Child*, Champaign, IL: Research Press

Ribbens McCarthy, J. (2006) *Young People's Experiences of Loss and Bereavement*, Maidenhead: Open University Press

Richardson, H., Davis, C. D. and Le May, A. (2001) 'A study of palliative day care using multiple case studies', *Palliative Medicine*, Vol. 15, pp. 524–5

Riches, G. and Dawson, P. (2000) *An Intimate Loneliness: Supporting Bereaved Parents and Siblings*, Buckingham: Open University Press

Robinson, S. (2008) *Spirituality, Ethics and Care*, London and F Kingsley Publishers

Rogers, C. R. (1951) *Client Centred Therapy*, London: Constable

Rolls, L. (2009) 'The ritual work of UK childhood bereavement ser Komaromy and C. Bartholomew (eds) (2009) *Death and Dying* Sage Publications, pp. 175– 83

Rumbold, B. (2002) 'From religion to spirituality', in B. Rumbold (ed and Palliative Care*, Melbourne: Oxford University Press, pp. 5–

Ryan, D. (2002) 'Spirituality – a Scottish healthcare issue', *Scottish Chaplaincy*, Vol. 5, No. 1, pp. 10–14

Salt, S. (1997) 'Towards a definition of suffering', *European Journal c 4, No. 2, pp. 58–60

Sandman, L. (2005) *A Good Death: on the Value of Death and Dying* University Press

Scottish Public Health Observatory (2008), 'Scotland overview repc ing profiles 2008', Public Health Information for Scotland

Seale, C. (1998) *Constructing Death: the Sociology of Dying and Bere Cambridge University Press

Seamark, D., Seamark, C. and Hynson, J. (2008) 'Life-limiting illne ence', in G. Mitchell (ed.) (2008) *Palliative Care: a Patient-Center Radcliffe Publishing, pp. 47–78

SEHD (2000) Working Party on Chaplaincy and Spiritual Care, *Scc Department*, Edinburgh: SEHD

SEHD (2004) 'Nursing people with cancer in Scotland: a framewc Health Department*, Edinburgh: SEHD

Sinclair, P. (2007) *Rethinking Palliative Care*, Bristol: The Policy P

Sinclair, S., Pereira, J. and Raffin, S. (2006) 'A thematic review of th within palliative care', *Palliative Medicine*, Vol. 9, No. 2, pp. 464

Smaje, C. and Field, D. (1997) 'Absent minorities? Ethnicity and th Services', in D. Field, J. Hockey and N. Small (eds) (1997) *Death London: Routledge, pp. 142–65

Smith, R. (2000) 'A good death', *British Medical Journal*, Vol. 320,

Sneddon, M. (2004) 'Specialist professional education in palliativ here and where are we going?', in S. Payne, J. Seymour and C. *Palliative Care Nursing*, Maidenhead: Open University Press, p

SPPC (2007) Scottish Partnership for Palliative Care, 'Palliative Scotland: the case for a cohesive approach', *Report and Recomm the Scottish Executive*, May 2007

SPPC (2009) Scottish Partnership for Palliative Care, www.palliat (accessed 18 May 2009)

Sque, M. and Payne, S. (2007) (eds) *Organ and Tissue Donatior Practice*, Maidenhead: Open University Press

Stoll, R. (1979) 'Guidelines for spiritual assessment', *America September, pp. 1574–5

Stroebe, M. S. and Schut, H. (1999) The dual process model of co rationale and description, *Death Studies*, Vol. 23, No. 3, pp. 19

Stroebe, W., Schut, H. and Stroebe. M. (2005) 'Grief work, disclos they help the bereaved?', *Clinical Psychology Review*, Vol. 25, p

Lawton, J. (2000) *The Dying Process: Patients' Experiences of Palliative Care*, London: Routledge

Leming, M. R. and Dickinson, G. E. (2007) *Understanding Dying, Death and Bereavement*, 6th edition, Belmont, CA: Thomson Higher Education

Lindemann, E. (1944) 'The symptomatology and management of acute grief', *American Journal of Psychiatry*, Vol. 101, pp. 141–8

Lofland, L. (1978) *The Craft of Dying: the Modern Face of Death*, Beverly Hills: Sage Publications

Low, J., Perry, R. and Wilkinson, S. (2005) 'A qualitative evaluation of the impact of palliative care day services: the experiences of patients, informal carers, day unit managers and volunteer staff', *Palliative Medicine*, Vol. 19, No. 1, pp. 65–70

Lucke, G., Gilbert, R. B. and Barrett, R. K. (2006) 'Protestant approaches to death: overcoming death's sting', in K. Garces-Foley (ed.) (2006) *Death and Religion in a Changing World*, Armonk, New York: M. E. Sharpe, pp. 122–46

MacLeod, R. (2008) 'Setting the context: what do we mean by psychosocial care in palliative care?', in M. Lloyd-Williams (ed.) (2008) *Psychosocial Issues in Palliative Care*, Oxford: Oxford University Press, pp. 1–20

Marie Curie (2004) http://campaign.mariecurie.org.uk

Marris, P. (1974) *Loss and Change*, London: Routledge Kegan Paul

Maslow, A. (1970) *Motivation and Personality*, New York: Harper & Row

Mason, T. and Whitehead, E. (2003) *Thinking Nursing*, Maidenhead: Open University Press

Mayne, M. (2006) *The Enduring Melody*, London: Darton, Longman and Todd

McGregor, S. (2002) 'Revised guidelines on chaplaincy and spiritual care in the NHS: synopsis of the report of the working party', *Scottish Journal of Healthcare Chaplaincy*, Vol. 5, No. 1, pp. 20–3

McIntosh, J. (1977) *Communication and Awareness in a Cancer Ward*, New York: Prodist

McMurray, A. (2004) 'Older people', in D. Oliviere and B. Monroe (eds) (2004) *Death, Dying and Social Differences*, Oxford: Oxford University Press, pp. 63–78

McSherry, W. (2000) *Making Sense of Spirituality in Nursing Practice*, London: Churchill Livingstone

McSherry, W. (2006) 'The principal components model: a model for advancing spirituality and spiritual care within nursing and health care practice', *Journal of Clinical Nursing*, Vol. 15, pp. 905–17

McSherry, W. and Cash, K. (2004) 'The language of spirituality: an emerging taxonomy', *International Journal of Nursing Studies*, Vol. 41, No. 2, pp. 151–61

Mitchell, G., Murray, J. and Hynson, J. (2008) 'Understanding the whole person: lifelimiting illness across the life cycle', in G. Mitchell (ed.) (2008) *Palliative Care: a Patient-Centered Approach*, Oxford: Radcliffe Publishing, pp. 79–108

Molyneux, D. (2007) 'And how is life going for you? – an account of subjective welfare in medicine', *Journal of Medical Ethics*, Vol. 33, pp. 568–82

Moore, J. and Purton, C. (eds) (2006) *Spirituality and Counselling: Experiential and Theoretical Perspectives*, Ross-on-Wye: PCCS Books

Mor, V., McHorney, C. and Sherwood, S. (1986) 'Secondary morbidity among the recently bereaved', *American Journal of Psychiatry*, Vol. 143, No. 2, pp. 158–63

Murray, S. A. and Sheikh, A. (2008) 'Making a difference: palliative care beyond cancer care for all at the end of life', *British Medical Journal*, Vol. 336, pp. 958–9

Myers, K. (2001) 'Future perspectives for day care', in J. Hearn and K. Myers (eds) (2001) *Palliative Day Care in Practice*, Oxford: Oxford University Press, pp. 136–52

Myers, K. and Hearn, J. (2001) 'An introduction to palliative day care: past and present', in J.Hearn and K. Myers (eds) (2001) *Palliative Day Care in Practice*, Oxford: Oxford University Press, pp. 1–11

Myrvold, K. (2006) 'Sikhism and death', in K. Garces-Foley (ed.) (2006) *Death and Religion in a Changing World*, Armonk, New York: M. E. Sharpe, pp. 178–204

Nagy, M. (1948) 'The child's theories concerning death', *Journal of Genetic Psychology*, Vol. 73, pp. 3–27

NHS End of Life Care Programme (2008), www.endoflifecareforadults.nhs.uk

NHS Scotland (2008) *Living and Dying Well: a National Action Plan for Palliative and End of Life Care in Scotland*, NHS Scotland, Edinburgh: The Scottish Government

NSO (2006) National Statistics Online, www.statistics.gov.uk

O'Connor, M. (2004) 'Transitions in status from wellness to illness, illness to wellness', in S. Payne, J. Seymour and C. Ingleton (eds) (2004) *Palliative Care Nursing Principles and Evidence for Practice*, Maidenhead: Open University Press, pp. 126–41

O'Keefe, K. (2001) 'Establishing day care', in J. Hearn and K. Myers (eds) (2001) *Palliative Day Care in Practice*, Oxford: Oxford University Press, pp. 43–58

Pargament, K. I., Murray-Swank, N. A. and Tarakeshwar, N. (2005) 'An empirically-based rationale for a spirituality-integrated psychotherapy', *Mental Health, Religion and Culture*, Vol. 8, No. 3, pp. 155–65

Parkes, C. M. (1988) 'Bereavement as a psychosocial transition: processes of adaptation to change', *Journal of Social Issues*, Vol. 44, No. 3, pp. 53–65

Parkes, C. M. (2000) 'Bereavement as a psychosocial transition: processes of adaptation to change', in D. Dickenson, M. Johnson and J. S. Katz (eds) (2000) *Death, Dying and Bereavement*, London: Sage Publications, pp. 325–31

Payne, S. and Seymour, J. (2004) 'Overview', in S. Payne, J. Seymour and C. Ingleton (eds) (2004) *Palliative Care Nursing*, Maidenhead: Open University Press, pp. 15–38

Peberdy, A. (2000) 'Spiritual care of dying people', in D. Dickenson, M. Johnson and J. S. Katz (eds) (2000) *Death, Dying and Bereavement*, London: Sage Publications, pp. 73–81

Pilgrim, D. (2006) *Real Life Issues: Bereavement*, Richmond, Surrey: Trotman and Company Ltd

Prior, L. (2000) 'The social distribution of sentiments', in D. Dickenson, M. Johnson and J. S. Katz (eds) (2000) *Death, Dying and Bereavement*, London: Sage Publications, pp. 332–7

Randall, F. and Downie, R. S. (2000) 'The main tradition', in D. Dickenson, M. Johnson and J. S. Katz (eds) *Death, Dying and Bereavement*, London: Sage Publications, pp. 263–9

Randall, F. and Downie, R. S. (2006) *The Philosophy of Palliative Care: Critique and Reconstruction*, Oxford: Oxford University Press

Rando, A. T. (1986) *Parental Loss of a Child*, Champaign, IL: Research Press

Ribbens McCarthy, J. (2006) *Young People's Experiences of Loss and Bereavement*, Maidenhead: Open University Press

Richardson, H., Davis, C. D. and Le May, A. (2001) 'A study of palliative day care using multiple case studies', *Palliative Medicine*, Vol. 15, pp. 524–5

Riches, G. and Dawson, P. (2000) *An Intimate Loneliness: Supporting Bereaved Parents and Siblings*, Buckingham: Open University Press

Robinson, S. (2008) *Spirituality, Ethics and Care*, London and Philadelphia: Jessica Kingsley Publishers

Rogers, C. R. (1951) *Client Centred Therapy*, London: Constable

Rolls, L. (2009) 'The ritual work of UK childhood bereavement services', in S. Earle, C. Komaromy and C. Bartholomew (eds) (2009) *Death and Dying: A Reader*, London: Sage Publications, pp. 175– 83

Rumbold, B. (2002) 'From religion to spirituality', in B. Rumbold (ed.) (2002) *Spirituality and Palliative Care*, Melbourne: Oxford University Press, pp. 5–21

Ryan, D. (2002) 'Spirituality – a Scottish healthcare issue', *Scottish Journal of Healthcare Chaplaincy*, Vol. 5, No. 1, pp. 10–14

Salt, S. (1997) 'Towards a definition of suffering', *European Journal of Palliative Care*, Vol. 4, No. 2, pp. 58–60

Sandman, L. (2005) *A Good Death: on the Value of Death and Dying*, Maidenhead: Open University Press

Scottish Public Health Observatory (2008), 'Scotland overview report: health and wellbeing profiles 2008', Public Health Information for Scotland

Seale, C. (1998) *Constructing Death: the Sociology of Dying and Bereavement*, Cambridge: Cambridge University Press

Seamark, D., Seamark, C. and Hynson, J. (2008) 'Life-limiting illness: the illness experience', in G. Mitchell (ed.) (2008) *Palliative Care: a Patient-Centered Approach*, Oxford: Radcliffe Publishing, pp. 47–78

SEHD (2000) Working Party on Chaplaincy and Spiritual Care, *Scottish Executive Health Department*, Edinburgh: SEHD

SEHD (2004) 'Nursing people with cancer in Scotland: a framework', *Scottish Executive Health Department*, Edinburgh: SEHD

Sinclair, P. (2007) *Rethinking Palliative Care*, Bristol: The Policy Press

Sinclair, S., Pereira, J. and Raffin, S. (2006) 'A thematic review of the spirituality literature within palliative care', *Palliative Medicine*, Vol. 9, No. 2, pp. 464–79

Smaje, C. and Field, D. (1997) 'Absent minorities? Ethnicity and the use of Palliative Care Services', in D. Field, J. Hockey and N. Small (eds) (1997) *Death, Gender and Ethnicity*, London: Routledge, pp. 142–65

Smith, R. (2000) 'A good death', *British Medical Journal*, Vol. 320, pp. 129–30

Sneddon, M. (2004) 'Specialist professional education in palliative care. How did we get here and where are we going?', in S. Payne, J. Seymour and C. Ingleton (eds) (2004) *Palliative Care Nursing*, Maidenhead: Open University Press, pp. 636–54

SPPC (2007) Scottish Partnership for Palliative Care, 'Palliative and end of life care in Scotland: the case for a cohesive approach', *Report and Recommendations submitted to the Scottish Executive*, May 2007

SPPC (2009) Scottish Partnership for Palliative Care, www.palliativecarescotland.org.uk (accessed 18 May 2009)

Sque, M. and Payne, S. (2007) (eds) *Organ and Tissue Donation: an Evidence Base for Practice*, Maidenhead: Open University Press

Stoll, R. (1979) 'Guidelines for spiritual assessment', *American Journal of Nursing*, September, pp. 1574–5

Stroebe, M. S. and Schut, H. (1999) The dual process model of coping with bereavement: rationale and description, *Death Studies*, Vol. 23, No. 3, pp. 197–224

Stroebe, W., Schut, H. and Stroebe. M. (2005) 'Grief work, disclosure and counselling: do they help the bereaved?', *Clinical Psychology Review*, Vol. 25, pp. 395–414

Swinton, J. (2001) *Spirituality and Mental Health: Rediscovering a 'Forgotten' Dimension*, London: Jessica Kingsley Publishers

Tanyi, R. A. (2002) 'Towards clarification of the meaning of spirituality', *Journal of Advanced Nursing*, Vol. 39, No. 5, pp. 500–9

Thompson, N. (1997) 'Masculinity and loss', in D. Field, J. Hockey and N. Small (eds) (1997) *Death, Gender and Ethnicity*, London: Routledge, pp. 76–88

Thompson, S. (2007) 'Spirituality and Old Age', *Illness, Crisis and Loss*, Vol. 15. No. 2, pp. 167–78

Thorne, B. (2005) *The Mystical Power of Person-centred Therapy: Hope beyond Despair*, London: Whurr Publishers Ltd

Tookman, A. J. and Scharpen-von Heussen, K. S. (2001) 'The role of the doctor in day care', in J. Hearn and K. Myers (eds) (2001) *Palliative Day Care in Practice*, Oxford: Oxford University Press, pp. 79–93

Twycross, R. (2003) *Introducing Palliative Care*, 4th edition, Abingdon: Radcliffe Medical Press

Vivat, B. (2008) '"Going down" and "getting deeper": physical and metaphorical location and movement in relation to death and spiritual care in a Scottish hospice', *Mortality*, Vol. 13, No. 1, pp. 42–64

von Hornstein, W. F. and Gruber, H. (2006) 'Art therapy and symptom control: a team approach', *European Journal of Palliative Care*, Vol. 13, No. 3, pp. 124–6

Walter, T. (1992) 'Modern death: taboo or not taboo?', *Sociology*, Vol. 25, No. 2, pp. 293–310

Walter, T. (1994) *The Revival of Death*, London: Routledge

Walter, T. (1996) 'A new model of grief: bereavement and biography', *Mortality*, Vol. 1, No. 1, pp. 7–25

Walter, T. (1997) 'The ideology and organization of spiritual care: three approaches', *Palliative Medicine*, Vol. 11, pp. 21–30

Walter, T. (1999) *On Bereavement: the Culture of Grief*, Maidenhead: Open University Press

Walter, T. (2002) 'Spirituality in palliative care: opportunity or burden?', *Palliative Medicine*, Vol. 16, No. 2, pp. 133–40

Walter, T. (2006) 'Disaster, modernity, and the media', in K. Garces-Foley (ed.) (2006) *Death and Religion in a Changing World*, Armonk, New York: M. E. Sharpe, pp. 265–82

Watts, J. H. (2008) 'Journeying with Morrie: challenging notions of professional delivery of spiritual care at the end of life', *Illness, Crisis and Loss*, Vol. 16, No. 4, pp. 305–19

Watts, J. H. (2009a) 'Being orphaned in early adulthood', in S. Earle, C. Bartholomew and C. Komaromy (eds) (2009) *Making Sense of Death, Dying and Bereavement: an Anthology*, London: Sage Publications, pp. 123–4

Watts, J. H. (2009b) '"I come because I can". Stories of hope from the cancer drop-in', *Illness, Crisis and Loss*, Vol. 17, No. 2, pp. 151–68

Watts, J. H. (2009c) 'Illness and the creative arts: a critical exploration', in S. Earle, C. Bartholomew and C. Komaromy (eds) (2009) *Death and Dying: a Reader*, London: Sage Publications, pp. 102–8

Watts, J. H. (2009d) 'Meanings of spirituality at the cancer drop-in', *International Journal of Qualitative Studies on Health and Well-being*, Vol. 4, No. 2, pp. 86–93

Weinstein, J. (2008) *Working with Loss, Death and Bereavement*, London: Sage Publications

Weisman, A. (1972) *On Dying and Denying*, New York: Behavioural Publications

White, G. (2006) *Talking about Spirituality in Health Care Practice*, London and Philadelphia: Jessica Kingsley Publishers

White, S. and Johnson, M. (2004) 'What do doctors actually do in the day hospice?', *European Journal of Palliative Care*, Vol. 11, No. 3, pp. 107–9

WHO (2002) *National Cancer Control Programmes: Policies and Managerial Guidelines*, 2nd edition, Geneva: World Health Organisation

Wilcock, A., Manderson, C., Weller, R., Walker, G., Carr, D., Carey, A-M., Broadhurst, D. and Mew, J. (2004) 'Does aromatherapy massage benefit patients with cancer attending a specialist palliative day care centre?', *Palliative Medicine*, Vol. 18, No. 4, pp. 287–90

Wilkes, E., Crowther, A. G. O. and Greaves, C. W. K. H. (1978) 'A different kind of day hospital for patients with preterminal cancer and chronic disease', *British Medical Journal*, Vol. 2, pp. 1053–6

Wilkinson, I. (2005) *Suffering: A Sociological Introduction*, Cambridge: Polity Press

Woods, S. (2007) *Death's Dominion: Ethics at the End of Life*, Maidenhead: Open University Press

Worden, J. W. (1982) *Grief Counselling and Grief Therapy: a Handbook for the Mental Health Practitioner*, New York: Springer

Worpole, K. (2009) *Modern Hospice Design*, Oxford: Taylor & Francis

Wright, M. (2004) 'Good for the soul? The spiritual dimension of hospice and palliative care', in S. Payne, J. Seymour and C. Ingleton (eds) (2004) *Palliative Care Nursing: Principles and Evidence for Practice*, Maidenhead: Open University Press, pp. 218–40

Wright, M., Wood, J., Lynch, T. and Clark, D. (2006) *Mapping Levels of Palliative Care Development: a Global View*, Lancaster: International Observatory on End of Life Care

Zohar, D. and Marshall, I. (2001) *SQ: Spiritual Intelligence, the Ultimate Intelligence*, London: Bloomsbury

Index